# BeagleBone Essentials

Harness the power of the BeagleBone Black to manage external environments using C, Bash, and Python/PHP programming

**Rodolfo Giometti**

open source*
community experience distilled

[PACKT]
PUBLISHING
BIRMINGHAM - MUMBAI

# BeagleBone Essentials

First published: May 2015

Production reference: 1260515

Published by Packt Publishing Ltd.
Livery Place
35 Livery Street
Birmingham B3 2PB, UK.

ISBN 978-1-78439-352-6

www.packtpub.com

Cover image by Andrea Dovichi (info@andreadovichi.com)

# Credits

**Author**

Rodolfo Giometti

**Reviewers**

Kumar Abhishek

Luca Belluomini

Richard Bottoms

Antonio Tringali

**Commissioning Editor**

Pramila Balan

**Acquisition Editor**

Subho Gupta

**Content Development Editor**

Samantha Gonsalves

**Technical Editor**

Siddhi Rane

**Copy Editor**

Rashmi Sawant

**Project Coordinator**

Kinjal Bari

**Proofreaders**

Stephen Copestake

Safis Editing

**Indexer**

Hemangini Bari

**Graphics**

Sheetal Aute

**Production Coordinator**

Komal Ramchandani

**Cover Work**

Komal Ramchandani

# About the Author

**Rodolfo Giometti** is an engineer, IT specialist, GNU/Linux expert, and software libre evangelist.

He is the maintainer of LinuxPPS projects (Linux's Pulse Per Second subsystem). He also actively contributes to the Linux source code community with several patches and new device drivers for industrial application devices.

He has over 20 years of experience working with x86, ARM, MIPS, and PowerPC-based platforms.

Now, he is the co-chief at HCE Engineering S.r.l. and a cofounder of the Cosino Project, which involves new hardware and software systems that are used for quick prototyping in the industry environment, control automation, and remote monitoring.

I would like to thank my wife, Valentina, for putting up with my late night writing sessions and my children, Romina and Raffaele, for reminding me to come back like a child from time to time during the job. I would also like to extend my deep thanks and gratitude to the Packt Publishing staff, especially Subho Gupta, who gave me the opportunity to write this book, Samantha Gonsalves, who helped me finish this book, and Siddhi Rane for her help in fixing my English. Many thanks to Armando Genovese for his help in fixing several electrical and hardware configuration issues. I would also like to thank Antonio Tringali, Luca Belluomini, and Kumar Abhishek for their support and efforts in reviewing this book so carefully.

I would also like to thank my mentor, Alessandro Rubini, who introduced me to the wonderful world of Linux device driver programming. Many thanks to Richard M. Stallman for the GNU Project and to Linus Torvalds for the Linux kernel.

Last but not least, I cannot forget to thank my parents, who gave me my first computer when I was a child and allowed me to be do what I do today.

# About the Reviewers

**Kumar Abhishek** is pursuing his integrated bachelor's and master's degree in electronics and electrical communication engineering at the Indian Institute of Technology, Kharagpur, India. He has worked with BeagleBoard.org under Google Summer of Code 2014 to develop BeagleLogic—a logic analyzer using the BeagleBone Black (for more information, visit `https://github.com/abhishek-kakkar/BeagleLogic/wiki`).

Abhishek wrote his first 8051 program when he was 11 years old, and since then, he has gained experience in a variety of embedded platforms, including 8051, AVR, STM32, and the BeagleBoard. His favorite toys as a child were his soldering iron and his computer, as he figured out that he could use them to build more awesome toys. When he isn't studying or working on his projects, he likes to read books and play the piano. Abhishek's personal abode on the Internet is "The Embedded Kitchen" at `www.theembeddedkitchen.net`.

I am grateful to my parents for nurturing and supporting my activities alongside academics. My project with BeagleBoard.org under Google Summer of Code in 2014 has been one of my most awesome experiences so far, and I'm fortunate to have had the privilege. I am excited at the opportunities awaiting makers exploring the realm of small but powerful platforms, such as the BeagleBoard, and I hope that this book will help in getting you up to speed.

**Luca Belluomini** is currently a member of AgustaWestland Technical Direction. He is in charge of fly control system design, certification, and testing for the AW609 TiltRotor integrated team, working between Italy (headquarters in Cascina Costa) and USA (Arlington, Texas) to certify the first civil TiltRotor aircraft with the Federal Aviation Administration.

Earlier in his career at Alenia Aermacchi, he worked for the M346 Master "Lead in Fighter" project and as a flight control law engineer in the Control Laws R&D team; he worked to ensure the safety of the flight test activities of the new generation dedicated to advanced and lead-in fighter trainer / light combat aircraft.

After passing the government exam and being licensed as a professional engineer, he served as an aeromechanical advisor for the "C27-J Spartan" Alenia Aeronautica program. He developed one of the few models of wind shear (an aerodynamic structure that characterizes the terrestrial boundary layer) integrated in a real-time level A full motion flight simulator to provide tools that are able to design and improve both take-off and landing procedures.

Luca received a bachelor's degree in aerospace science and a master's degree in aeronautical science from Università degli Studi di Pisa.


**Richard Bottoms** is a former US Army Signal Corps NCO and is now a San Francisco Bay Area-based developer of innovative software and hardware technologies.

His website design and development work began in the Internet's earliest days, when he developed one of the country's first media publication websites with database-backed classified systems for Nuvo Newsweekly, Indianapolis, Indiana (`http://www.nuvo.net/`).

He came to California to take up a management role with one of the first firms built to service Fortune 500 clients at Santa Clara, based US Web, honing some of the first enterprise-level best practices for the Internet while upgrading the art of technical sales.

Later, he led the technical sales team for Agniroth, a leading Indian firm offering offshore support to Silicon Valley firms with their value proposition of a 24-hour development cycle, allowing nonstop innovations with command and control in the US.

Following the dot-com crash, the freedom of open source with low cost, high benefit technologies such as LAMP (Linux Apache MySQL PHP) allowed him to survive it by building lightweight, agile support mechanisms for surviving firms evolving from the breakdown.

In 2007, he took a chance with an untested technology, choosing the unproven iPhone over the dominant Palm, Inc., and their growing line of Treo mobile phones. Obviously, this was the right choice as iPhone became the first true smartphone and its operating system iOS has changed the world.

Later in 2012, recognizing new technologies that were gaining importance, he began working on the integration of Arduino-compatible microcontrollers projects using Bluetooth Smart, which was introduced with iPhone 4S.

Now a mature technology, BLE (Bluetooth Low Energy) has led to the well-known meme the Internet of Things (IoT), which has spawned exciting interconnected smart technologies that link social networking tools with location-aware smart TCP/IP addressable devices.

He hopes to make a significant contribution in this field before retiring with his wonderful wife back in Germany, where he once served as a soldier, before he found his calling in the field of computing.

**Antonio Tringali** is an electronic engineer working as a freelancer, who specializes in automation and remote system control. Most of his work in recent years is concentrated on automated parking systems and train passenger information systems. He develops everything a client may throw at him—from the silicon up to the database—alternating a number of computer languages with the oscilloscope.

He likes to read as much as he can about, well, everything. He likes to write and teach, so it should not be surprising that he started to know and appreciate Rodolfo when both were writing for the same leading Italian Linux magazine.

I would like to thank my parents, as they allowed me to fly away to catch my dreams by the tail. I would also like to thank my wonderful wife and sons for keeping me anchored to the stuff that really matters a lot in my life—the best dream you may want to catch.

# www.PacktPub.com

## Support files, eBooks, discount offers, and more

For support files and downloads related to your book, please visit www.PacktPub.com.

Did you know that Packt offers eBook versions of every book published, with PDF and ePub files available? You can upgrade to the eBook version at www.PacktPub.com and as a print book customer, you are entitled to a discount on the eBook copy. Get in touch with us at service@packtpub.com for more details.

At www.PacktPub.com, you can also read a collection of free technical articles, sign up for a range of free newsletters and receive exclusive discounts and offers on Packt books and eBooks.

https://www2.packtpub.com/books/subscription/packtlib

Do you need instant solutions to your IT questions? PacktLib is Packt's online digital book library. Here, you can search, access, and read Packt's entire library of books.

## Why subscribe?

- Fully searchable across every book published by Packt
- Copy and paste, print, and bookmark content
- On demand and accessible via a web browser

## Free access for Packt account holders

If you have an account with Packt at www.PacktPub.com, you can use this to access PacktLib today and view 9 entirely free books. Simply use your login credentials for immediate access.

# Table of Contents

# Preface

The BeagleBone Black is an embedded system that is able to run an embedded GNU/Linux distribution as well as a normal (and powerful) distribution, such as Debian or Ubuntu, and where the user can connect several external peripherals to it via two dedicated expansion connectors.

By having a powerful distribution capability with an easily expandable embedded board, the BeagleBone black system is a state-of-the-art device that allows you to build powerful and versatile monitoring and controlling applications.

Packed with real-world examples, this book will try to fill the gap by showing you how some peripherals can be connected to the BeagleBone Black, and how you can get access to them in order to develop your own monitoring and control systems.

After the introductory chapter about how to set up the board from scratch, we'll take a look at compilation and cross-compilation of both user space and kernel space applications with some basic debugging techniques. Next, we'll move to high-level applications, such as daemons, and high-level programming using scripting languages, such as PHP, Python, and Bash. Finally, we'll see how a system daemon works and how it can be implemented from scratch using several programming languages.

This book will also explain how several computer peripherals can be connected to the BeagleBone Black board. We'll present several kinds of devices, such as serial ports, USB host ports and devices, and SPI/I²C/1-Wire devices. For each peripheral, we'll see how it can be connected to the BeagleBone Black, and how the developer can get access to it from the user space, and in some circumstances we'll see some kernel code too.

The hardware is presented in a generic manner, so no BeagleBone Black capes are presented in this book! This is because each cape has tons of documentation on the Internet, and using a generic approach allows you to better understand how the hardware management works and how to replicate the examples on another GNU/Linux-based system with a little effort.

Accessing all peripherals and writing good monitoring and controlling programs can both be complex tasks; it's easy to make mistakes early in the development stage that leads to serious problems in production. Learning the best practices before starting your project will help you avoid these problems and ensure that your project will be a success.

# What this book covers

*Chapter 1, Installing the Developing System*, shows you how to use the BeagleBone Black's on-board operating system and how to (re)install and set up a complete developing system, based on the Debian distribution, starting from zero.

*Chapter 2, Managing the System Console*, shows you how a serial console works, and how you can use it in order to control/monitor the system activities (that is, monitoring the kernel messages, managing the bootloader, and so on). At the end of this chapter, a special section will introduce you to some bootloader commands.

*Chapter 3, Compiling versus Cross-compiling*, show you all the compiling steps in both kernel and user space to easily add a new driver that is not included in the standard BeagleBone Black's kernel and/or to recompile a user-space tool, which is not included in the Debian distribution.

*Chapter 4, Quick Programming with Scripts*, shows you how to install and use some common scripting languages in the BeagleBone Black board, and then how to solve a real problem by writing the solution in each language, in order to show you the differences between the usage of these languages.

*Chapter 5, Device Drivers*, shows you a possible implementation of a very simple driver (by writing a proper kernel module), in order to show you some basics of the Linux kernel's internals.

*Chapter 6, Serial Ports and TTY Devices*, discusses the serial ports, which is one of the most important peripheral classes a computer can have. We'll see how we can manage them in a Linux system in order to use a real serial device.

*Chapter 7, Universal Serial Bus – USB*, shows you how the USB bus works, the different types of USB devices and how they are supported in the BeagleBone Black's kernel. Simple management examples of real USB device and USB gadget are present.

*Chapter 8, Inter-integrated Circuit – I²C*, shows you how the I²C bus works, giving you a panoramic view, as wide as possible, of the most commonly used I²C devices; we'll discuss an EEPROM, a DAC, and an ADC.

*Chapter 9, Serial Peripheral Interface – SPI*, shows you how the SPI bus works by presenting you a simple temperature sensor management, as a quite complex device, such as a mini LCD display.

*Chapter 10, 1-Wire Bus – W1*, shows you how the 1-Wire bus works by showing you how to get access to a temperature sensor.

*Chapter 11, Useful System Daemons*, discusses the Unix daemon by showing you how an embedded computer developer can use existing daemons or new written ones in several programming languages.

# What you need for this book

The prerequisites required for efficient learning are mentioned in the following sections.

## Software prerequisites

You should have a little knowledge of the software of a non-graphical text editor, such as vi, emacs, or nano. You can even connect an LCD display, a keyboard, and a mouse directly to the BeagleBone Black, and then use the graphical interface; in this book, we assume that you are able to do little modifications to the text files using a text-only editor.

The host computer, that is, the computer you will use to cross-compile the code and/or to manage the BeagleBone Black is assumed to run on a GNU/Linux-based distribution. My host PC is running an Ubuntu 14.04 LTS, but you can use a Debian-based system too with little modification, or you may use another GNU/Linux distribution but with a little effort from you, mainly regarding cross-compiling tools installation. Foreign systems, such as Windows, Mac OS, or similar ones, are not covered in this book because we should not use low technology systems to develop the code for high technology systems.

To know how a C compiler works and how to manage a Makefile could help, but don't worry, all examples start from the very beginning, so even a developer who is not skilled should be able do the job.

This book will present some kernel programming techniques but these cannot be taken as a *kernel programming course*. You need a proper book for such a topic! However, each example is well-documented and you will find several suggested resources.

Finally, let me add that knowing a visualization system could be useful, especially in case you wish to set up your own developing host computer.

# Hardware prerequisites

In this book, all the code is developed for the BeagleBone Black board Revision C, but you can use an older revision without any issues; in fact, the code is portable, and it should work on other systems too!

The computer peripherals used in this book are discussed in the section where I got the hardware and where you can buy it; but of course, you can decide to surf the Internet in order to find a better and cheaper offer.

You should not have any difficulties connecting the hardware to the BeagleBone Black presented in this book, since the connections are very few and well documented. They don't require any particular hardware skills to be performed by you.

# Who this book is for

If you are a developer who wants to learn how to use embedded machine learning capabilities and get access to a GNU/Linux device driver to collect data from a peripheral or to control a device, this is the book for you. If you have some hardware or electrical engineering experience and know the basics of C, Bash, and Python/PHP programming in a Unix environment but desire to learn more about it, then this book is for you.

# Conventions

In this book, you will find a number of text styles that distinguish between different kinds of information. Here are some examples of these styles and an explanation of their meaning.

# Codes and command lines

Code words in text, database table names, folder names, filenames, file extensions, pathnames, dummy URLs, user input, and Twitter handles are shown as follows: "To get the preceding kernel messages, we can use both the `dmesg` and `tail -f /var/log/kern.log` commands."

A block of code is set as follows:

```c
#include <stdio.h>

int main(int argc, char *argv[])
{
```

```
        printf("Hello World!\n");

        return 0;
}
```

When we wish to draw your attention to a particular part of a code block, the relevant lines or items are set in bold:

```
#include <stdio.h>

int main(int argc, char *argv[])
{
        printf("Hello World!\n");

        return 0;
}
```

Any command line input or output given on the BeagleBone Black is written as follows:

```
root@BeagleBone:~# make CFLAGS="-Wall -O2" helloworldcc -Wall -O2
helloworld.c -o helloworld
```

Any command line input or output given on my host computer as a *non-privileged user* is written as follows:

```
$ tail -f /var/log/kern.log
```

When I need to give a command as a privileged user (root) on my host computer the command line input or output is then written as follows:

```
# /etc/init.d/apache2 restart
```

The reader should notice that all privileged commands can be executed by a normal user too by using the sudo command with the form:

```
$ sudo <command>
```

So the preceding command can be executed by a normal user as:

```
$ sudo /etc/init.d/apache2 restart
```

# Kernel and logging messages

On several GNU/Linux distribution a kernel message has the usual form:

```
Oct 27 10:41:56 hulk kernel: [46692.664196] usb 2-1.1: new high-speed USB
device number 12 using ehci-pci
```

Which is a quite long line for this book, that's why the characters from the start of the lines till the point where the real information begin are dropped. So, in the preceding example, the lines output will be reported as follow:

```
usb 2-1.1: new high-speed USB device number 12 using ehci-pci
```

Long outputs, repeated or less important lines in a terminal are dropped by replacing them with three dots . . . shown as follows:

```
output begin

output line 1

output line 2

...

output line 10

output end
```

# File modifications

When the reader should modify a text file, I'm going to use the *unified context diff* format since this is a very efficient and compact way to represent a text modification. This format can be obtained by using the `diff` command with the `-u` option argument.

As a simple example, let's consider the following text into `file1.old`:

```
This is first line
This is the second line
This is the third line
...
...
This is the last line
```

Suppose we have to modify the third line as highlighted in the following snippet:

```
This is first line
This is the second line
This is the new third line modified by me
...
...
This is the last line
```

The reader can easily understand that reporting each time the whole file for a simple modification it's quite obscure and space consuming, however by using the *unified context diff* format the preceding modification can be written as follow:

```
$ diff -u file1.old file1.new
```

```
--- file1.old 2015-03-23 14:49:04.354377460 +0100
+++ file1.new 2015-03-23 14:51:57.450373836 +0100
@@ -1,6 +1,6 @@
 This is first line
 This is the second line
-This is the third line
+This is the new third line modified by me
 ...
 ...
 This is the last line
```

Now the modification is very clear and written in a compact form! It starts with a two-line header where the original file is preceded by --- and the new file is preceded by +++, then follows one or more change hunks that contain the line differences in the file. The preceding example has just one hunk where the unchanged lines are preceded by a space character, while the lines to be added are preceded by a + character and the lines to be removed are preceded by a - character.

# Other conventions

**New terms** and **important words** are shown in bold. Words that you see on the screen, for example, in menus or dialog boxes, appear in the text like this: "If it prints **Hello World**, then our code has been executed successfully!"

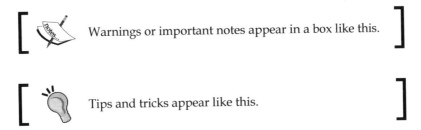

Warnings or important notes appear in a box like this.

Tips and tricks appear like this.

# Reader feedback

Feedback from our readers is always welcome. Let us know what you think about this book—what you liked or disliked. Reader feedback is important for us as it helps us develop titles that you will really get the most out of.

To send us general feedback, simply e-mail feedback@packtpub.com, and mention the book's title in the subject of your message.

If there is a topic that you have expertise in and you are interested in either writing or contributing to a book, see our author guide at www.packtpub.com/authors.

# Customer support

Now that you are the proud owner of a Packt book, we have a number of things to help you to get the most from your purchase.

# Downloading the example code

You can download the example code files from your account at `http://www.packtpub.com` for all the Packt Publishing books you have purchased. If you purchased this book elsewhere, you can visit `http://www.packtpub.com/support` and register to have the files e-mailed directly to you.

For this book, the example code can also be downloaded from the author's GitHub repository at URL `https://github.com/giometti/beaglebone_essentials`.

Just use the following command to get it at once:

```
$ git clone https://github.com/giometti/beaglebone_essentials.git
```

The examples are grouped according to the chapters name so you can easily find the code during the reading of the book.

# Downloading the color images of this book

We also provide you with a PDF file that has color images of the screenshots/diagrams used in this book. The color images will help you better understand the changes in the output. You can download this file from `https://www.packtpub.com/sites/default/files/downloads/3526OS_ColoredImages.pdf`.

# Errata

Although we have taken every care to ensure the accuracy of our content, mistakes do happen. If you find a mistake in one of our books—maybe a mistake in the text or the code—we would be grateful if you could report this to us. By doing so, you can save other readers from frustration and help us improve subsequent versions of this book. If you find any errata, please report them by visiting `http://www.packtpub.com/submit-errata`, selecting your book, clicking on the **Errata Submission Form** link, and entering the details of your errata. Once your errata are verified, your submission will be accepted and the errata will be uploaded to our website or added to any list of existing errata under the Errata section of that title.

To view the previously submitted errata, go to `https://www.packtpub.com/books/content/support` and enter the name of the book in the search field. The required information will appear under the **Errata** section.

# Piracy

Piracy of copyrighted material on the Internet is an ongoing problem across all media. At Packt, we take the protection of our copyright and licenses very seriously. If you come across any illegal copies of our works in any form on the Internet, please provide us with the location address or website name immediately so that we can pursue a remedy.

Please contact us at copyright@packtpub.com with a link to the suspected pirated material.

We appreciate your help in protecting our authors and our ability to bring you valuable content.

# Questions

If you have a problem with any aspect of this book, you can contact us at questions@packtpub.com, and we will do our best to address the problem.

# 1

# Installing the Developing System

In this first chapter, after a short introduction to some common terms of the embedded programming used in this book, we'll give you a brief overview of BeagleBone Black's hardware features, how to use the BeagleBone Black's on-board operating system, and how to (re)install and set up a complete developing system based on the Debian distribution, starting from zero. At the end of this chapter, we will give you some hints on how to install a complete host system based on Ubuntu.

## Embedded world terms

Before putting our hands on our new board, it is recommended that we acquaint ourselves with some terms that the user should know in order to avoid misunderstandings. People who have already worked with some GNU/Linux and/or embedded systems may skip this part; however, a brief overview of these preliminary stuff may be useful for everyone. The BeagleBone Black is a tiny single-board computer that can be embedded into a device, so the user should be familiar with some terms used in the wonderful world of the embedded programming.

| Term | Description |
|---|---|
| Target | The target system is the embedded computer that we wish to manage. Usually, it is an ARM platform, but this is not a fixed rule; in fact, PowerPC and MIPS are other (less) common platforms. Even the x86 platform (a standard PC) can be an embedded computer too. |

| Term | Description |
|------|-------------|
| **Host** | The host system is the computer we will use to manage the target system. Usually, it is a normal PC (x86 platform) but even other platforms can be used (for example, years ago, I used a PowerPC-based computer as a host PC). |
| | Normally, the host system is more powerful than the target one since it's usually used for heavy compiling tasks that the target cannot do at all or that it can do but in a time consuming manner. |
| **Serial console** | This is the most important communication port in an embedded system. Using the serial console, the user has complete control of the system. Since it's not only indispensable for debugging, but is also the last resort if, by chance, the operating system files are messed up and the board refuses to boot. |
| | Without the serial console, the user can still control the system (if correctly set up) but for the developer/debugger it's a must-have! |
| **Native compiler** | The native compiler is just a-compiler! This is the compiler running on a machine (host or target) that builds the code for the current machine (that is, the compiler running on a PC builds the code for the PC like the one running on an ARM machine that builds the code for ARM itself). |
| **Cross-compiler** | Strictly speaking, the cross-compiler is just a compiler that builds the code for a foreign platform (that is, a cross-compiler can run on a PC in order to generate binaries for an ARM platform), but usually, by using this term, the embedded developers also mean the complete compilation suite, that is: the compiler, linker, binutils, libc, and so on. |

# A system overview

The BeagleBone Black is a complete computer despite its dimensions. In fact, it's a little bigger than a credit card yet power packed.

The main hardware key features are as follows:

| Part | Specification |
|------|---------------|
| Processor | ARM processor: Sitara AM3358 @ 1 Ghz with 3D engine |
| SDRAM memory | 512 MB DDR3 @800 Mhz |
| On-board flash | 4 GB, 8-bit eMMC |
| USB 2.0 ports | 1 device |
| | 1 host |
| Serial port | UART0 via 6 pin 3.3 V TTL connector |
| Ethernet | 10/100 via RJ45 connector |

| Part | Specification |
|------|---------------|
| SD/MMC | MicroSD 3.3 V slot |
| Video out | 16b HDMI 1280 x 1024 |
| Audio out | Stereo via HDMI interface |
| LED indicators | <ul><li>1 for power</li><li>2 on the Ethernet port</li><li>4 user controllable</li></ul> |
| Expansion connectors | <ul><li>Power 5 V, 3.3 V, VDD ADC (1.8 V)</li><li>69 (max) GPIOs 3.3 V</li><li>SPI, I²C, LCD, GPMC, MMC1-2, CAN</li><li>7 ADC (1.8 V max)</li><li>4 timers</li><li>4 serial ports</li><li>3 PWMs</li></ul> |

The following image shows a top view of the BeagleBone Black, where we can see some interesting things:

- The connector **J1** can be used to access the serial console (this concept will be explained in detail in the *Getting access to the serial console* section of *Chapter 2, Managing the System Console*).
- The Ethernet connector.
- The two expansion connectors **P8** and **P9**, where we can connect the dedicated extension boards and/or custom peripherals (these connectors will be explained in detail in the next chapters).
- The **reset** button can be used to reset the board. The **power** button can be used to turn on/off the board.

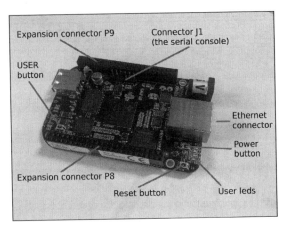

From the preceding image, we can see that the BeagleBone Black doesn't look like a PC, but it can act as a PC! The BeagleBone Black is a fully functional single-board computer and can be readily used as a PC if required by connecting a monitor to the HDMI port and attaching a USB keyboard and mouse through a USB hub. However, it is more suited to embedded applications, where it can act as more than a PC due its expansion connectors, and we can stack up to four expansion boards (named **capes**) that are useful for several purposes.

In this book, we'll see how we can manage (and reinstall) a complete Debian distribution that allows us to have a wide set of ready-to-run software packages, as a normal PC may have (in fact, the Debian ARM version is equivalent to the Debian x86 version). Then, we'll see how we can use the expansion connectors to connect to the board. Several peripherals are used to monitor/control the external environment.

# The first login

Once we get our new BeagleBone Black in front of us, we just have a board and a USB cable, so the only thing to do is to connect one end of the USB cable to the BeagleBone Black's mini USB connector and the other end to our PC's USB host port:

If everything works well, we should see the BeagleBone Black's user LEDs blinking (on the board, these LEDs are labeled as **USER LEDS**) and after a while, on the host PC, we should get some kernel messages as follows:

```
usb 2-1.1: new high-speed USB device number 12 using ehci-pci
usb 2-1.1: New USB device found, idVendor=1d6b, idProduct=0104
usb 2-1.1: New USB device strings: Mfr=2, Product=3, SerialNumber=4
usb 2-1.1: Product: BeagleBoneBlack
usb 2-1.1: Manufacturer: Circuitco
```

```
usb 2-1.1: SerialNumber: C0-3214BBBK0716
rndis_host 2-1.1:1.0 eth0: register 'rndis_host' at usb-0000:00:1d.0-1.1,
RNDIS device, 78:a5:04:ca:cb:00
cdc_acm 2-1.1:1.2: This device cannot do calls on its own. It is not a
modem.
cdc_acm 2-1.1:1.2: ttyACM0: USB ACM device
```

 I'm using an Ubuntu 14.04 LTS-based system as a host PC. To get the preceding kernel messages, we can use both the `dmesg` and `tail -f /var/log/kern.log` commands.

This behavior means that the BeagleBone Black is working correctly, so let's first log in to the system.

Let's take a look at the preceding kernel messages. We will notice the following two lines:

```
cdc_acm 2-1.1:1.2: This device cannot do calls on its own. It is not a
modem.
cdc_acm 2-1.1:1.2: ttyACM0: USB ACM device
```

The serial device `ttyACM0` can be used to get access to the BeagleBone Black's internal system. To do so, we can use a terminal emulator; usually, I use `minicom`, but you can use your preferred tool. In case of `minicom`, the following command line is used:

```
$ minicom -o -D /dev/ttyACM0
```

You must now verify that the serial port setup is `115200,8N1` without the hardware and software flow control (in `minicom`, these settings can be checked using the *Ctrl +A + O* key sequence, and then selecting the entry in the **Serial port setup** menu).

Now, if we press the *Enter* key, we get the following string:

```
Password:
```

Nothing to worry about, just hit the *Enter* key again and then enter the string `root` when the board asks for an user account as reported as follows:

```
BeagleBone login:
```

No password is needed here. The console then displays the last login time and the version. It will look something like this:

```
Last login: Wed Apr 23 20:20:54 UTC 2014 on ttyGS0
Linux BeagleBone 3.8.13-bone47 #1 SMP Fri Apr 11 01:36:09 UTC 2014 armv7l

The programs included with the Debian GNU/Linux system are free software;
```

```
the exact distribution terms for each program are described in the
 individual files in /usr/share/doc/*/copyright.


Debian GNU/Linux comes with ABSOLUTELY NO WARRANTY, to the extent
permitted by applicable law.
root@BeagleBone:~#
```

Great! We just did our first login!

# Checking out the preloaded tools

Now that we are logged into the system, it's time to take a look at the preloaded tools. In the next section, we're going to install all the missing software that a good developing system needs.

# The SSH tool

Now we should verify that the **Secure Shell (SSH)** tool is functional. The Secure Shell, sometimes known as Secure Socket Shell, is a Unix-based command interface for securely getting access to a remote computer. It was designed to replace the insecure telnet. To test it on the target serial console, we can use the `ifconfig` command to check the network settings:

```
root@BeagleBone:~# ifconfig
```

Then, the following message is displayed:

```
eth0      Link encap:Ethernet  HWaddr 78:a5:04:ca:c9:fe
          UP BROADCAST MULTICAST  MTU:1500  Metric:1
          RX packets:0 errors:0 dropped:0 overruns:0 frame:0
          TX packets:0 errors:0 dropped:0 overruns:0 carrier:0
          collisions:0 txqueuelen:1000
          RX bytes:0 (0.0 B)  TX bytes:0 (0.0 B)
          Interrupt:40


lo        Link encap:Local Loopback
          inet addr:127.0.0.1  Mask:255.0.0.0
          inet6 addr: ::1/128 Scope:Host
          UP LOOPBACK RUNNING  MTU:65536  Metric:1
```

```
             RX packets:0 errors:0 dropped:0 overruns:0 frame:0
             TX packets:0 errors:0 dropped:0 overruns:0 carrier:0
             collisions:0 txqueuelen:0
             RX bytes:0 (0.0 B)  TX bytes:0 (0.0 B)


usb0         Link encap:Ethernet  HWaddr 96:66:68:88:3b:fa
             inet addr:192.168.7.2  Bcast:192.168.7.3  Mask:255.255.255.252
             inet6 addr: fe80::9466:68ff:fe88:3bfa/64 Scope:Link
             UP BROADCAST RUNNING MULTICAST  MTU:1500  Metric:1
             RX packets:3376 errors:0 dropped:0 overruns:0 frame:0
             TX packets:41 errors:0 dropped:0 overruns:0 carrier:0
             collisions:0 txqueuelen:1000
             RX bytes:926304 (904.5 KiB)  TX bytes:10306 (10.0 KiB)
```

We can use the usb0 device (which is a virtual Ethernet running on the USB cable).
First, we should check whether the corresponding Ethernet device has been created
on the host using the same command:

```
$ ifconfig
```

The output of the command is as follows:

```
eth1         Link encap:Ethernet  HWaddr bc:ae:c5:20:36:80
             UP BROADCAST MULTICAST  MTU:1500  Metric:1
             RX packets:0 errors:0 dropped:0 overruns:0 frame:0
             TX packets:0 errors:0 dropped:0 overruns:0 carrier:0
             collisions:0 txqueuelen:1000
             RX bytes:0 (0.0 B)  TX bytes:0 (0.0 B)


eth4         Link encap:Ethernet  HWaddr 78:a5:04:ca:cb:00
             inet addr:192.168.7.1  Bcast:192.168.7.3  Mask:255.255.255.252
             inet6 addr: fe80::7aa5:4ff:feca:cb00/64 Scope:Link
             UP BROADCAST RUNNING MULTICAST  MTU:1500  Metric:1
             RX packets:112 errors:0 dropped:0 overruns:0 frame:0
             TX packets:3483 errors:0 dropped:0 overruns:0 carrier:0
             collisions:0 txqueuelen:1000
             RX bytes:17031 (17.0 KB)  TX bytes:1143213 (1.1 MB)
```

Note that I dropped all the network devices that are not named `ethX` (for example, the `lo` device, `wlanX`, and so on.).We can notice that the `eth4` device, which owns the IP address `192.168.7.1`, is the one we are looking for. Because of this fact, its IP address is in the same subnet of the BeagleBone Black's `usb0` device mentioned earlier. So, let's get connected via SSH to our board with the following command:

```
$ ssh root@192.168.7.2
```

```
The authenticity of host '192.168.7.2 (192.168.7.2)' can't be
established.
ECDSA key fingerprint is b1:a9:84:39:71:99:a3:af:9e:ba:26:d5:e6:77:03:08.
Are you sure you want to continue connecting (yes/no)? yes
Warning: Permanently added '192.168.7.2' (ECDSA) to the list of known
hosts.
Debian GNU/Linux 7


BeagleBoard.org BeagleBone Debian Image 2014-04-23


Support/FAQ: http://elinux.org/Beagleboard:BeagleBoneBlack_Debian
Last login: Thu Apr 24 21:20:09 2014 from hulk.local
root@BeagleBone:~#
```

Great! We can now be rest assured that the SSH is working.

We have to answer `yes` when the `ssh` command asks us if we are sure we want to continue.

# The Apache web server

In the Internet era, a web interface is a *must-have*, and the easy way to have one is to install a **LAMP (Linux-Apache-MySQL-PHP)** suite.

By default, the preloaded Debian image has the Apache web server preinstalled, so if we point our web browser to the host at the address `192.168.7.2` and port `8080`, we should get something like this:

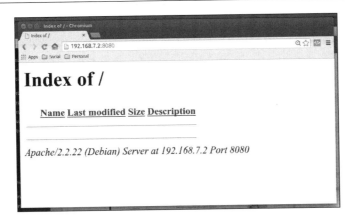

However, we must not forget to mention the port 8080 specification in the URL (the correct form is 192.168.7.2:8080), or we'll get a different output related to the Bone101 service, as shown in the following screenshot:

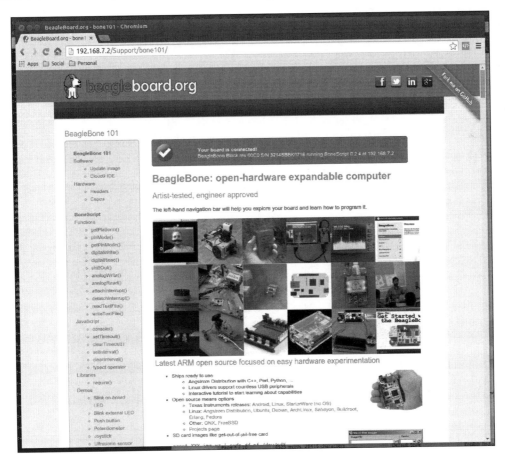

The Bone101 service is something similar to the Arduino IDE, which is a high-level programming environment, where beginners can try simple programs using an integrated IDE and a dedicated JavaScript library.

You can take a look at this system using the tutorial at `http://beagleboard.org/support/bone101`. However, we are going to disable this service in the next section because it's not useful to better understand how the computer peripherals can be connected to and managed by the BeagleBone Black, and also, in order to get a standard LAMP suite, we need port `80` to be free.

# Setting up a developing system

Ok, first of all, we should set up the networking settings, since we are going to download a lot of software packages. The Ethernet cable should be plugged into the BeagleBone Black's Ethernet connector and the other end should be connected to the LAN switch. If the connection works, we should see the following line in the BeagleBone Black's kernel messages:

```
libphy: 4a101000.mdio:00 - Link is Up - 100/Full
```

Let me remind you that you can use either the `tail -f /var/log/kern.log` or dmesg command to see the kernel messages.

We can avoid using an Ethernet connection with a network trick; in fact, the host PC can be used as a gateway, for the BeagleBone Black, that can access the Internet using the USB cable. In the host, we can use the following commands:

```
# iptables --table nat --append POSTROUTING --out-interface eth1 -j MASQUERADE
# iptables --append FORWARD --in-interface eth4 -j ACCEPT
# echo 1 >> /proc/sys/net/ipv4/ip_forward
```

Then, on the BeagleBone Black, we can set the gateway through the USB cable using the following command:

```
root@beaglebone:~# route add default gw 192.168.7.1
```

The eth1 device is the preferred Internet connection on the host system, while the eth4 device is the BeagleBone Black's device as viewed on the host system, as already seen earlier.

If we have a DHCP server installed in our LAN, the `eth0` interface should automatically display an IP address. Here is what I get on my LAN:

```
root@BeagleBone:~# ifconfig eth0
eth0        Link encap:Ethernet  HWaddr 78:a5:04:ca:c9:fe
            inet addr:192.168.32.30  Bcast:192.168.32.255 Mask:255.255.255.0
            inet6 addr: fe80::7aa5:4ff:feca:c9fe/64 Scope:Link
            UP BROADCAST RUNNING MULTICAST  MTU:1500  Metric:1
            RX packets:143 errors:0 dropped:0 overruns:0 frame:0
            TX packets:136 errors:0 dropped:0 overruns:0 carrier:0
            collisions:0 txqueuelen:1000
            RX bytes:23623 (23.0 KiB)  TX bytes:19576 (19.1 KiB)
            Interrupt:40
```

However, if the DHCP server is up and running, but for some mystic reasons, this magic doesn't happen, we can force it using the following command:

```
root@BeagleBone:~# dhclient eth0
```

On the other hand, if the DHCP server is not working at all, we can use a static configuration by altering the `/etc/network/interfaces` file by adding the following lines:

```
iface eth0 inet static
    address 192.168.32.30
    netmask 255.255.255.0
    network 192.168.32.0
    gateway 192.168.32.8
```

Next, we need to add the DNS settings to the `/etc/resolv.conf` file by adding the following lines:

```
nameserver 94.249.192.104
nameserver 8.8.8.8
```

 Note that the IP/DHCP addresses mentioned in the commands are user specific. You should change them so that they match your settings.

When all the modifications are in place, we should restart the networking activities:

```
root@BeagleBone:~# /etc/init.d/networking restart
```

Now we are ready to verify that the network settings are set correctly by trying to update the software repositories with the following command:

```
root@BeagleBone:~# aptitude update
Get: 1 http://security.debian.org wheezy/updates Release.gpg [836 B]
Get: 2 http://ftp.us.debian.org wheezy Release.gpg [1,655 B]
Get: 3 http://debian.beagleboard.org wheezy-bbb Release.gpg [490 B]
Get: 4 http://security.debian.org wheezy/updates Release [102 kB]
...
Get: 38 http://ftp.us.debian.org wheezy-updates/main 2014-06-16-2054.31.pdiff [5
01 B]
Fetched 20.1 MB in 35s (561 kB/s)


Current status: 78 updates [+78], 2 new [+2].
There is 1 newly obsolete package: libmozjs10d
```

Here, the system tells you that just one package is obsolete, and there are some new packages to be installed, so you can either leave all of them untouched or decide to upgrade everything. In the latter case, we can use the following command:

```
root@BeagleBone:~# aptitude upgrade
The following packages will be upgraded:
  acpi-support-base apache2 apache2-mpm-worker apache2-utils apache2.2-bin
  apache2.2-common apt apt-utils base-files bash BeagleBone bind9-host curl
  dbus dbus-x11 dpkg dpkg-dev file gnupg gpgv libapt-inst1.5 libapt-pkg4.12
  libavcodec-dev libavcodec53 libavformat-dev libavformat53 libavutil-dev
  libavutil51 libbind9-80 libc-bin libc-dev-bin libc6 libc6:armel libc6-dev
  libcups2 libcurl3 libcurl3-gnutls libdbus-1-3 libdbus-1-dev libdns88
  libdpkg-perl libgnutls26 libgssapi-krb5-2 libisc84 libisccc80 libisccfg82
  libjpeg-progs libjpeg8 libjpeg8-dev libk5crypto3 libkrb5-3
  libkrb5support0 liblcms2-2 liblwres80 libmagic1 libnspr4 libnss3
  libsmbclient libsoup-gnome2.4-1 libsoup2.4-1 libssl-dev libssl-doc
  libssl1.0.0 libswscale-dev libswscale2 libwbclient0 libxfont1 libxml2
  libxml2-dev libxml2-utils linux-libc-dev locales multiarch-support
  openssh-client openssh-server openssl rsyslog tzdata
The following packages are RECOMMENDED but will NOT be installed:
  bash-completion gnupg-curl gnupg-curl:armel krb5-locales
```

```
78 packages upgraded, 0 newly installed, 0 to remove and 0 not upgraded.
Need to get 53.2 MB of archives. After unpacking 159 kB will be freed.
Do you want to continue? [Y/n/?]
```

A lot to do here. For the moment, I decide to leave the system untouched. So, I just answer no by typing *n*.

# The LAMP suite

Now let's see how to set up a proper LAMP suite.

## Apache

First of all, we should drop the Bone101 service in order to free port 80, which is the World Wide Web's default port:

```
root@BeagleBone:~# systemctl stop bonescript.socket
root@BeagleBone:~# systemctl disable bonescript.socket
rm '/etc/systemd/system/sockets.target.wants/bonescript.socket'
```

Ok. Now, to test whether port 80 is really free, we type the following command and echo it to be sure of its status:

```
root@BeagleBone:~# netstat -pln | grep ':80\>' || echo "OK."
OK.
```

Now, we can switch the Apache web server from port 8080 to port 80 by altering the first lines of the /etc/apache2/sites-enabled/000-default file as follows:

```
--- 000-default.orig  2014-04-23 20:21:56.619140638 +0000
+++ 000-default  2014-10-10 20:00:21.752090984 +0000
@@ -1,4 +1,4 @@
-<VirtualHost *:8080>
+<VirtualHost *:80>
    ServerAdmin webmaster@localhost

    DocumentRoot /var/www
```

Then, replace all the 8080 occurrences with the string 80 in the /etc/apache2/ports.conf file as follows:

```
--- ports.conf.orig  2014-04-23 20:23:46.623046902 +0000
+++ ports.conf  2014-04-23 20:24:01.580078153 +0000
@@ -5,8 +5,8 @@
 # Debian etch). See /usr/share/doc/apache2.2-common/NEWS.Debian.gz
and
```

```
# README.Debian.gz

-NameVirtualHost *:80
-Listen 80
+NameVirtualHost *:8080
+Listen 8080

<IfModule mod_ssl.c>
      # If you add NameVirtualHost *:443 here, you will also have to
change
```

Now that all the modifications are done, we will now restart the server. To do so, we will use the following command:

```
root@BeagleBone:~# /etc/init.d/apache2 restart
[....] Restarting apache2 (via systemctl): apache2.service. ok
```

Once the server has been restarted, we will check whether the server is in the listening state. To do this, we will type the following command:

```
root@BeagleBone:~# netstat -pln | grep ':80\>'
tcp6       0       0 :::80                           :::*             LISTEN
2367/apache2
```

Ok, we did it! You can now repoint your browser to the default port 80 to verify that everything is working correctly.

# PHP

Now, we can verify that the Apache PHP support is working by adding a simple PHP file to the DocumentRoot directory /var/www, as specified in the /etc/apache2/sites-enabled/000-default configuration file:

```
root@BeagleBone:~# cd /var/www/
root@BeagleBone:/var/www# cat > test.php <<EOF
<?php
phpinfo();
?>
EOF
```

> The <<EOF trick used in the preceding command is often used when we need to supply one or more commands to a program directly to its standard input line (stdin). Using such a syntax, we tell the Bash shell to send the lines to the command itself and the line that holds the EOF characters directly to stdin of the executed command.

Now, if we point the browser to the URL http://192.168.7.2/test.php, we'll most probably get a blank page. This means that Apache lacks the PHP support, so let's install it:

```
root@BeagleBone:~# aptitude install libapache2-mod-php5 apache2-mpm-
worker- apache2-
The following NEW packages will be installed:
  apache2-mpm-prefork{a} libapache2-mod-php5 libonig2{a} libqdbm14{a}
  lsof{a} php5-cli{a} php5-common{a}
The following packages will be REMOVED:
  apache2 apache2-mpm-worker
The following packages will be upgraded:
  apache2.2-bin apache2.2-common
2 packages upgraded, 7 newly installed, 2 to remove and 74 not upgraded.
Need to get 6,748 kB of archives. After unpacking 14.4 MB will be used.
Do you want to continue? [Y/n/?]
```

Don't forget the sign—after apache2-mpm-worker and apache2 because this means that we want to uninstall these packages, as they are incompatible with the apache2-mpm-prefork package.

You may discover the difference between the apache2-mpm-worker and apache2-mpm-prefork packages by surfing the net.

Let's press *y* and proceed:

```
Get: 1 http://ftp.us.debian.org/debian/ wheezy/main lsof armhf 4.86+dfsg-1 [315
kB]
Get: 2 http://security.debian.org/ wheezy/updates/main php5-common armhf 5.4.4-1
4+deb7u14 [589 kB]...
Setting up php5-common (5.4.4-14+deb7u14) ...
Setting up apache2-mpm-prefork (2.2.22-13+deb7u3) ...
[....] Starting apache2 (via systemctl): apache2.service. ok
Setting up libonig2 (5.9.1-1) ...
Setting up libqdbm14 (1.8.78-2) ...
Setting up libapache2-mod-php5 (5.4.4-14+deb7u14) ...

Creating config file /etc/php5/apache2/php.ini with new version
[....] Restarting apache2 (via systemctl): apache2.service. ok
Setting up php5-cli (5.4.4-14+deb7u14) ...
```

We can update the alternatives using /usr/bin/php5 to provide /usr/bin/php (php) in auto mode. Note that during this procedure, we may get a lot of errors, which are as follows:

```
insserv: Starting led_aging.sh depends on rc.local and therefore on system facil
ity `$all' which can not be true!
insserv: Max recursions depth 99 reached
insserv:  loop involving service udhcpd at depth 2
insserv: There is a loop between service rc.local and mountall-bootclean if star
ted...
dpkg: error processing apache2-mpm-worker (--configure):
 dependency problems - leaving unconfigured
Errors were encountered while processing:
 apache2.2-common
 apache2
 apache2-mpm-worker
```

Don't panic! Just replace the /etc/init.d/led_aging.sh file with the following code:

```
#!/bin/sh -e
### BEGIN INIT INFO
# Provides:           led_aging.sh
# Required-Start:     $local_fs
# Required-Stop:      $local_fs
# Default-Start:      2 3 4 5
# Default-Stop:       0 1 6
# Short-Description: Start LED aging
# Description:        Starts LED aging (whatever that is)
### END INIT INFO

x=$(/bin/ps -ef | /bin/grep "[l]ed_acc")
if [ ! -n "$x" -a -x /usr/bin/led_acc ]; then
  /usr/bin/led_acc &
fi
```

**Downloading the example code**

You can download the example code files from your account at http://www.packtpub.com for all the Packt Publishing books you have purchased. If you purchased this book elsewhere, you can visit http://www.packtpub.com/support and register to have the files e-mailed directly to you.

Ok. Now we can test the PHP support by reloading the URL `http://192.168.7.2/test.php`. The output should be something similar to the following screenshot:

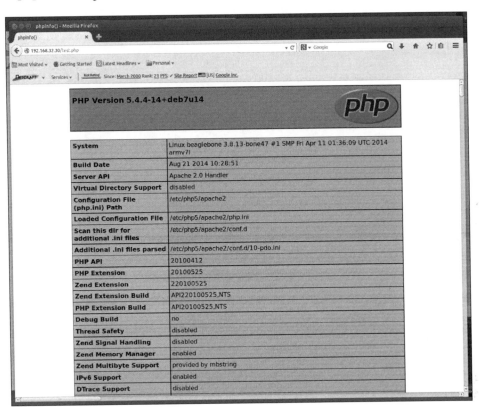

# MySQL

Now the last step is to add the MySQL database server and the corresponding PHP support.

Installing the MySQL server is quite easy:

```
root@BeagleBone:~# aptitude install mysql-server mysql-client
```

Installing the Developing System

Type the preceding command and proceed with the installation as mentioned earlier, and when the system asks for an administrative password for the database of the root user (don't confuse this MySQL user with the system's root user!), we should create one.

> It may happen that some strange characters are displayed on the serial terminal; don't panic, it's just a display issue. We can ignore them and enter the desired root's password.
>
> Also, note that you can install the `mysql-client` packet too to be able to manage the database settings from the command line.

When finished, the system should display this:

```
Setting up libhtml-template-perl (2.91-1) ...
Setting up mysql-client (5.5.38-0+wheezy1) ...
Setting up mysql-server (5.5.38-0+wheezy1) ...
```

This means that the MySQL server is up and running. We can easily test it by running the following command, again using the preceding <<EOF trick:

```
root@BeagleBone:~# mysql -u root -p <<EOF
show databases;
EOF
```

The system will ask for the database's root password to be inserted during the installation by showing the following line:

```
Enter password:
```

Then, if the password is correct, the output will be as follows:

```
Database
information_schema
mysql
performance_schema
```

If we get the preceding output, it means that we did it! This means that the installation was successful. However, the PHP still lacks the MySQL support; in fact, if we add the following code to the `mysql_test.php` file in the `/var/www` directory (as done earlier for the `test.php` file):

```php
<?php
        # Check the PHP's MySQL support
```

[18]

```
if (!function_exists("mysql_connect"))
        die("MySQL support missing!");

# Get connect with the MySQL server.
# Don't forget to replace the following string "ROOTPASS" with
# the database's root password you choose during the installation!!!
$connect = mysql_connect("localhost", "root", "ROOTPASS")
        or die("Unable to Connect");
mysql_select_db("information_schema")
        or die("Could not open the db");

# Do a simple query
$showtablequery = "SHOW TABLES FROM information_schema";
$query_result = mysql_query($showtablequery);

# Let's display the result!
while($row = mysql_fetch_array($query_result))
        echo $row[0] . " ";
?>
```

Then, pointing the web browser to the URL `http://192.168.32.30:8080/mysql_test.php`, we will see an error message as follows:

**MySQL support missing!**

So, to install PHP's MySQL support, use the following command:

**root@BeagleBone:~# aptitude install php5-mysql**

If we try reloading the preceding URL, we will not see the error messages anymore but the following text:

```
CHARACTER_SETS COLLATIONS COLLATION_CHARACTER_SET_APPLICABILITY COLUMNS
COLUMN_PRIVILEGES ENGINES EVENTS FILES GLOBAL_STATUS GLOBAL_VARIABLES
KEY_COLUMN_USAGE PARAMETERS PARTITIONS PLUGINS PROCESSLIST PROFILING
REFERENTIAL_CONSTRAINTS ROUTINES SCHEMATA SCHEMA_PRIVILEGES SESSION_
STATUS SESSION_VARIABLES STATISTICS TABLES TABLESPACES TABLE_CONSTRAINTS
TABLE_PRIVILEGES TRIGGERS USER_PRIVILEGES VIEWS INNODB_BUFFER_PAGE
INNODB_TRX INNODB_BUFFER_POOL_STATS INNODB_LOCK_WAITS INNODB_CMPMEM
INNODB_CMP INNODB_LOCKS INNODB_CMPMEM_RESET INNODB_CMP_RESET INNODB_
BUFFER_PAGE_LRU
```

# The compiler

Just a few years ago, the native compilation of programs on the target embedded system was previously unheard of, but the latest CPUs are now really powerful and both the RAM and storage (Flash, MMC, and so on.) memories are quite large to support native compilations. The BeagleBone hardware is capable of handling native compilations with ease although in terms of compilation time, it is more practical to cross-compile for larger projects or use the kernel (that's why we will show you how to install a cross-compiler on the host PC in the last section of this chapter).

The command to install the GGC suite is as follows:

```
root@BeagleBone:~# aptitude install gcc make
```

On my system, the preceding packages are already installed; in this case, the preceding command will give an answer to us as follows:

```
No packages will be installed, upgraded, or removed.
0 packages upgraded, 0 newly installed, 0 to remove and
74 not upgraded.
Need to get 0 B of archives. After unpacking 0 B will
be used.
```

To check whether the compiler is working, we can consider compiling the classic *Hello World* C program. To do so, just insert the following code into a file called helloworld.c:

```c
#include <stdio.h>

int main(int argc, char *argv[])
{
        printf("Hello World!\n");

        return 0;
}
```

Now we can compile it using the following command:

```
root@BeagleBone:~# make CFLAGS="-Wall -O2" helloworld
cc -Wall -O2    helloworld.c   -o helloworld
```

To execute the new program, type the following line:

```
root@BeagleBone:~# ./helloworld
```

Hello World! If it prints **Hello World**, then our code has been executed successfully!

# (Re)Installing Debian

The on-board system is a complete *ready-to-use* Debian distribution; however, it may happen that we may need another image (maybe during some developing stages) or just for backup purposes (just in case, the default image is corrupted for some reason). So, it's important to see how we can install an alternate image on our board.

There are many ways to install a Debian OS on our BeagleBone Black. I'm going to use the simplest and quickest one using a prebuild image to be put on a microSD. This solution has the advantage that by simply removing the microSD from the system, the board will boot with the original default image.

[ A similar procedure may be used to install a different OS too. Note that the microSD should be a class 10 and have at least 4 GB storage space. ]

The first step is to download the image to a working directory on the host machine. We have several resources on the Internet, but I chose the one at `http://ynezz. ibawizard.net/beagleboard/wheezy/`.

The command to download the file is as follows:

```
$ wget http://ynezz.ibawizard.net/beagleboard/wheezy/debian-7.6-console-armhf-2014-08-13.tar.xz
```

By the time you read this, new versions could be available or the current one could be missing. Then, you should verify the available versions in case of errors while downloading the `rootfs` image used earlier. Next, unzip it, and then enter the newly created directory:

```
$ tar xf debian-7.6-console-armhf-2014-08-13.tar.xz
$ cd debian-7.6-console-armhf-2014-08-13
```

We are now ready to build our microSD.

[ This is a very important step! Follow the steps carefully or you may damage your host system. ]

The command to build the microSD is as follows:

```
# ./setup_sdcard.sh --mmc /dev/sdX --dtb BeagleBone
```

Here the `/dev/sdX` device must be chosen carefully. The best way to do so is using the tail command on the host in order to watch the kernel messages while we insert the microSD into our host PC:

```
$ tail -f /var/log/kern.log
```

In this situation, an usual kernel activity should be something like this:

```
usb 2-1.1: new high-speed USB device number 18 using ehci-pci
usb 2-1.1: New USB device found, idVendor=058f, idProduct=6387
usb 2-1.1: New USB device strings: Mfr=1, Product=2, SerialNumber=3
usb 2-1.1: Product: Miss Storage
usb 2-1.1: Manufacturer: Generic
usb 2-1.1: SerialNumber: 9B4B5BCC
usb-storage 2-1.1:1.0: USB Mass Storage device detected
scsi13 : usb-storage 2-1.1:1.0
scsi 13:0:0:0: Direct-Access     Generic  Flash Disk      8.07 PQ: 0 ANSI: 2
sd 13:0:0:0: Attached scsi generic sg3 type 0
sd 13:0:0:0: [sdd] 15663104 512-byte logical blocks: (8.01 GB/7.46 GiB)
sd 13:0:0:0: [sdd] Write Protect is off
sd 13:0:0:0: [sdd] Mode Sense: 03 00 00 00
sd 13:0:0:0: [sdd] No Caching mode page found
sd 13:0:0:0: [sdd] Assuming drive cache: write through
sd 13:0:0:0: [sdd] No Caching mode page found
sd 13:0:0:0: [sdd] Assuming drive cache: write through
 sdd: sdd1
sd 13:0:0:0: [sdd] No Caching mode page found
sd 13:0:0:0: [sdd] Assuming drive cache: write through
sd 13:0:0:0: [sdd] Attached SCSI removable disk
FAT-fs (sdd1): Volume was not properly unmounted. Some data may be corrupt.
Please run fsck.
```

If we take a look at the preceding messages, it is quite clear that on my PC, the device used is `/dev/sdd`. In fact, these lines tell me that the newly attached SCSI device (the microSD) has been assigned to the `sdd` device.

Depending on our system configuration, we may discover that the right device to use is /dev/sdb, /dev/sdc, and so on or even a device named as /dev/mmcblk0. In this last case, our host PC is using a MMC device instead of a USB adapter to manage the SD or microSD slot of the PC. In this special situation, the kernel messages look like:

```
mmc0: cannot verify signal voltage switch
mmc0: new ultra high speed SDR50 SDHC card at address
0007
mmcblk0: mmc0:0007 SD4GB 3.70 GiB
mmcblk0: p1
```

Once the right device has been discovered, we can proceed with the microSD creation:

```
# ./setup_sdcard.sh --mmc /dev/sdd --dtb BeagleBone
```

The system will display a complete disk configuration asking for user confirmation; if we are sure about what we are doing, we've simply to answer yes and go on. At the end, we should see something like this:

```
Debug: image has: v3.16.0-armv7-x4
Debug: image has: v3.16.0-armv7-lpae-x2
Debug: image has: v3.8.13-bone63
Debug: using: v3.8.13-bone63
Finished populating rootfs Partition
-----------------------------
setup_sdcard.sh script complete
-----------------------------
The default user:password for this image:
debian:temppwd
-----------------------------
```

Well, now we can remove the microSD from the host PC and put it in our BeagleBone Black. If everything has been done correctly, then after we reboot, we can log in to our new Debian system in the same way as we did during our first login earlier:

```
$ minicom -o -D /dev/ttyACM0
```

Note that this time, we have to wait a bit longer that the normal boot due to some configuration issues of this Debian image, which can delay the booting time. This fact will be more clear in the following chapter, where we will be able to see the serial console messages.

Then, as reported, at the end of the microSD creation stage, we must supply the `debian` user with the `temppwd` password (don't worry if no login prompt is displayed), as shown in the following code:

```
debian
Password:
Last login: Wed Apr 23 20:21:01 UTC 2014 on ttyGS0
Linux BeagleBone 3.8.13-bone47 #1 SMP Fri Apr 11 01:36:09 UTC 2014 armv7l


The programs included with the Debian GNU/Linux system are free software;
the exact distribution terms for each program are described in the
individual files in /usr/share/doc/*/copyright.


Debian GNU/Linux comes with ABSOLUTELY NO WARRANTY, to the extent
permitted by applicable law.
debian@BeagleBone:~$
```

# The virtual machine

As stated at the beginning of this book, as a host system, I'm using a normal PC running Ubuntu 14.04 LTS distribution. Those who may wish to use another GNU/Linux-based OS can use most of the commands I'm going to use in the next chapter without any modifications (or with just a few differences, these can be replaced with a little effort). However, those who still insist on using a Windows- or Mac OS-based host system may have some troubles in following what I do, that's why I decided to write this little section/tutorial to help these people to install a GNU/Linux host system on their computers.

The trick to do our job is quite simple: we should use a virtual machine! Here, it is not so important to know which visualization system is used (my preference is for VirtualBox), the important thing is to install a GNU/Linux-based OS.

I will skip the instructions on how to install a new OS on a virtual machine since this is not the purpose of this book and because this operation is quite simple.

# Setting up the host

Ok, now that our new GNU/Linux OS is running on our new virtual machine, we need to make some adjustments in order to use it as a real host PC.

 All the commands are for Ubuntu 14.04 LTS. You should use the proper commands if you decide to install a different GNU/Linux distribution.

First of all, let's check the networking settings; we should verify that our system can access the Internet so that we can install all the needed tools.

## The serial connection

To check whether we can get connected to our BeagleBone via the emulated serial port, as we did during our first login, we need to install the `minicom` tool:

```
bbb@bbb-VirtualBox:~$ sudo apt-get install minicom
```

After the installation is completed, verify that the virtual machine is connected to the USB host port, where the BeagleBone Black is connected by checking the kernel messages as done earlier:

```
cdc_acm 1-1:1.2: ttyACM0: USB ACM device
```

You should verify that the USB device corresponding to the BeagleBone Black is connected to the virtual machine. This action depends on the virtual machine implementation used, and it implies some actions taken by the user. For example, VirtualBox allows you to choose the serial port from a menu, otherwise it stays connected to the host. Great! The serial port is accessible, so let's use the `minicom` command:

```
bbb@bbb-VirtualBox:~$ sudo minicom -o -D /dev/ttyACM0
```

 Note that on Ubuntu, an unprivileged user may need the `sudo` command to get access to the `/dev/ttyACM0` device.

Also, we should verify that the serial connection settings are set, as during our first login, this is `115200,8N1`, without both hardware and software flow controls.

# The Ethernet connection

Now let's check the Ethernet connection emulated via the USB cable. Using the `ifconfig` command, we can check whether the Ethernet devices are up and running on both the host and target systems. On the host, we have the following:

```
bbb@bbb-VirtualBox:~$ ifconfig eth1
eth1      Link encap:Ethernet   HWaddr 78:a5:04:ca:cb:00
          inet addr:192.168.7.1  Bcast:192.168.7.3  Mask:255.255.255.252
          inet6 addr: fe80::7aa5:4ff:feca:cb00/64 Scope:Link
          UP BROADCAST RUNNING MULTICAST  MTU:1500  Metric:1
          RX packets:2 errors:0 dropped:0 overruns:0 frame:0
          TX packets:53 errors:0 dropped:0 overruns:0 carrier:0
          collisions:0 txqueuelen:1000
          RX bytes:580 (580.0 B)  TX bytes:11465 (11.4 KB)
```

Depending on the virtual machine configuration, the Ethernet device `ethX` may vary, so we can use the `ifconfig` command without any arguments in order to get a list of all the networking devices present on the system. So, recalling what we did before, we should get connected to the target using the `ssh` command from the host system:

```
bbb@bbb-VirtualBox:~$ ssh root@192.168.7.2
The authenticity of host '192.168.7.2 (192.168.7.2)' can't be
established.
ECDSA key fingerprint is b1:a9:84:39:71:99:a3:af:9e:ba:26:d5:e6:77:03:08.
Are you sure you want to continue connecting (yes/no)? yes
Warning: Permanently added '192.168.7.2' (ECDSA) to the list of known
hosts.
Debian GNU/Linux 7


BeagleBoard.org BeagleBone Debian Image 2014-04-23


Support/FAQ: http://elinux.org/Beagleboard:BeagleBoneBlack_Debian
Last login: Wed Apr 23 20:20:26 2014
root@BeagleBone:~#
```

Ok, everything is working correctly!

# The developing tools

In the end, the only tool that we need on the host is the C cross-compiler suite.

It can be installed using the following command on the newly created virtual machine:

```
$ sudo apt-get install gcc-arm-linux-gnueabihf make
```

Now we can try to compile the previous *Hello World* C example program on our new virtualized host PC:

```
$ make CC=arm-linux-gnueabihf-gcc CFLAGS="-Wall -O2" cross-helloworld
arm-linux-gnueabihf-gcc -Wall -O2    cross-helloworld.c    -o cross-
helloworld
```

 Note that now I've renamed the preceding *Hello World* program to `cross-helloworld.c` and the command line is quite different from before. The options of the `make` command are needed to select the cross-compiler and to use special compilation flags.

Now we can check whether the cross-compiler did its job correctly using the `file` command as follows:

```
bbb@bbb-VirtualBox:~$ file cross-helloworld
cross-helloworld: ELF 32-bit LSB  executable, ARM, EABI5 version 1
(SYSV), dynamically linked (uses shared libs), for GNU/Linux 2.6.32, Buil
dID[sha1]=5ea2036028d983438e38fc2df1a21d24d8fd7e59, not stripped
```

Yes, our cross-compiler is a good guy, but to be completely sure, we should test the code on our BeagleBone Black by copying the binary to it:

```
bbb@bbb-VirtualBox:~$ scp cross-helloworld root@192.168.7.2:
Debian GNU/Linux 7

BeagleBoard.org BeagleBone Debian Image 2014-04-23

Support/FAQ: http://elinux.org/Beagleboard:BeagleBoneBlack_Debian
cross-helloworld                          100% 8357      8.2KB/s
00:00
```

We will then execute it on the target:

```
bbb@bbb-VirtualBox:~$ ssh root@192.168.7.2 ./cross-helloworld
Debian GNU/Linux 7

BeagleBoard.org BeagleBone Debian Image 2014-04-23

Support/FAQ: http://elinux.org/Beagleboard:BeagleBoneBlack_Debian
Hello World!
```

> In the last command, we used `ssh` to execute the `cross-helloworld` binary file on the remote machine to display the result on the local machine.
>
> You can read more about this feature in the `ssh` user manual at `http://www.openssh.com/manual.html`.

# Summary

In this chapter, we first logged in to our new BeagleBone Black, and then we set up all the developing tools we are going to use in the next chapters (the LAMP suite, native compiler, cross-compiler, and so on).

However, before we start using them, we need to do a fundamental step: we need to get access to the serial console in order to be able to get full control of our embedded board. This topic is presented in the next chapter.

# 2
# Managing the System Console

In this chapter, you will learn how a serial console works, and how you can use it in order to control/monitor the system activities (for example, monitoring the kernel messages, managing the bootloader, and so on).

Then, a brief introduction of the basic system management commands will be presented. In this section, you will learn about some useful command-line tools to manipulate files, and how to manage the distribution's packages.

At the end of the chapter, a special section will introduce you to the bootloader commands so that you may feel more confident to manage this important component of the system.

## Getting access to the serial console

As shown in *Chapter 1, Installing the Developing System*, during our first login, we can easily get access to the system through a USB connection; however, doing it this way we use a virtual serial line created by the kernel that is not available during the first boot stages (that is, when the bootloader runs).

However, to have more control of the board (that is, complete booting stage control, kernel debugging messages, and so on), we must get access to the serial console, which is a real device, and it can be accessed using a serial adapter connected to connector **J1**, as shown in the following image:

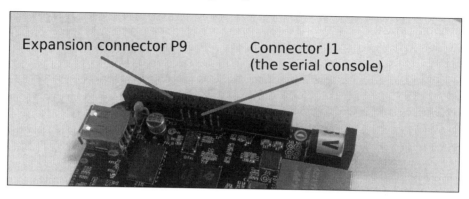

There are two different kinds of serial adapters on the market. The first one is a standard FTDI USB to TTL cable, as shown in the following image:

While the second one is a standard TTL to RS232 converter, as shown in the following image:

 The TTL to RS232 converter can be purchased (or by surfing the Internet) at
`http://www.cosino.io/product/rs-232-serial-adapter`.

In both the cases, we have to carefully read the device pinout, and then connect the adapter with the BeagleBone Black's connector **J1**, according to the following pin functions:

| Connector J1 | Function | Adapter pin |
|--------------|----------|-------------|
| Pin 2 | CTS | n.c. |
| Pin 4 | TXD | RXD |
| Pin 5 | RXD | TXD |
| Pin 6 | RTS | n.c. |

 Note that you must pay attention to the fact that the TXD pin is connected to the RXD pin, while CTS and RTS can be left unconnected.

Warning! There exists two kinds of these devices: the 3.3 V version and the 5 V version. You must be sure to have the 3.3 V version.

However, one main difference exists. If we use the FTDI USB to TTL cable, we don't need to connect the Vcc pin, and the GND pin must be connected to the connector **J1**, as shown in the following table:

| Connector J1 | Function |
|---|---|
| Pin 1 | GND |

However, if we use the TTL to RS232 adapter, we need a supply voltage that can be taken from the expansion connector **P9**, as shown in the following table:

| Connector P9 | Function |
|---|---|
| Pin 1 | GND |
| Pin 3 | Vcc 3.3 V |

When all the preceding connections are in place, we can turn on the board, and from the serial line, we should be able see the following booting stage messages:

```
U-Boot SPL 2014.04-00014-g47880f5 (Apr 22 2014 - 13:23:54)

reading args

spl_load_image_fat_os: error reading image args, err - -1

reading u-boot.img

reading u-boot.img
```

These preceding messages are related to the prebootloader that is used to initialize the CPU and the system's RAM, where the prebootloader will store the real bootloader.

The boot then continues with the following bootloader messages:

```
U-Boot 2014.04-00014-g47880f5 (Apr 22 2014 - 13:23:54)


I2C:    ready
DRAM:   512 MiB
NAND:   0 MiB
MMC:    OMAP SD/MMC: 0, OMAP SD/MMC: 1
*** Warning - readenv() failed, using default environment
```

These messages tell us that the bootloader is U-Boot, while the following messages show us some system settings:

```
Net:    <ethaddr> not set. Validating first E-fuse MAC
cpsw, usb_ether
```

```
Hit any key to stop autoboot:   0
gpio: pin 53 (gpio 53) value is 1
Card did not respond to voltage select!
mmc0(part 0) is current device
Card did not respond to voltage select!
```

In the following messages, we can see that there is no card inserted in the microSD slot (the slot is named as mmc0):

```
gpio: pin 56 (gpio 56) value is 0
gpio: pin 55 (gpio 55) value is 0
gpio: pin 54 (gpio 54) value is 0
mmc1(part 0) is current device
gpio: pin 54 (gpio 54) value is 1
SD/MMC found on device 1
```

While these messages tell us that the on-board eMMC is fully functional, so U-Boot will read the kernel image from them:

```
reading uEnv.txt
1430 bytes read in 5 ms (279.3 KiB/s)
gpio: pin 55 (gpio 55) value is 1
Loaded environment from uEnv.txt
Importing environment from mmc ...
```

 Note that even if both microSD and eMMC are mass storage memories, the microSD is a card that the user can insert or remove from the system, while the eMMC is an on-board chip.

Now the bootloader starts reading some settings in order to configure the kernel properly:

```
Checking if uenvcmd is set ...
gpio: pin 56 (gpio 56) value is 1
Running uenvcmd ...
reading zImage
3717760 bytes read in 205 ms (17.3 MiB/s)
reading initrd.img
2869101 bytes read in 160 ms (17.1 MiB/s)
```

```
reading /dtbs/am335x-boneblack.dtb
25080 bytes read in 8 ms (3 MiB/s)
Kernel image @ 0x82000000 [ 0x000000 - 0x38ba80 ]
## Flattened Device Tree blob at 88000000
    Booting using the fdt blob at 0x88000000
    Using Device Tree in place at 88000000, end 880091f7


Starting kernel ...
```

Now the bootloader is ready to safely start the kernel! Note that to simplify the reading all booting messages are taken verbatim from the serial console.

```
Uncompressing Linux... done, booting the kernel.
[    0.382635] omap2_mbox_probe: platform not supported
[    0.549475] tps65217-bl tps65217-bl: no platform data provided
[    0.614599] bone-capemgr bone_capemgr.9: slot #0: No cape found
[    0.651706] bone-capemgr bone_capemgr.9: slot #1: No cape found
[    0.688814] bone-capemgr bone_capemgr.9: slot #2: No cape found
[    0.725923] bone-capemgr bone_capemgr.9: slot #3: No cape found
[    0.742074] bone-capemgr bone_capemgr.9: slot #6: BB-BONELT-HDMIN conflict P8
.45 (#5:BB-BONELT-HDMI)
[    0.751670] bone-capemgr bone_capemgr.9: slot #6: Failed verification
[    0.758424] bone-capemgr bone_capemgr.9: loader: failed to load slot-6 BB-BON
ELT-HDMIN:00A0 (prio 2)
[    0.774920] omap_hsmmc mmc.5: of_parse_phandle_with_args of 'reset' failed
[    0.837530] pinctrl-single 44e10800.pinmux: pin 44e10854 already requested by
 44e10800.pinmux; cannot claim for gpio-leds.8
[    0.849243] pinctrl-single 44e10800.pinmux: pin-21 (gpio-leds.8) status -22
[    0.856525] pinctrl-single 44e10800.pinmux: could not request pin 21 on devic
e pinctrl-single
```

Here the kernel has started and the root filesystem is being mounted:

```
Loading, please wait...
Scanning for Btrfs filesystems


systemd-fsck[202]: rootfs: clean, 77153/230144 files, 410755/919296
blocks
```

```
Debian GNU/Linux 7 BeagleBone ttyO0

default username:password is [debian:temppwd]

Support/FAQ: http://elinux.org/Beagleboard:BeagleBoneBlack_Debian

The IP Address for usb0 is: 192.168.7.2
BeagleBone login:
```

Great! At this point, the boot stages are completed and the system asks for the login.

 Note that to get the messages from the serial console, I used `minicom`, as in *The first login* section of *Chapter 1, Installing the Developing System,* through the `/dev/ttyUSB0` device instead of the `/dev/ttyACM0` device (but the reader configuration may vary according to the USB adapter used).

Let me explain the main difference between the two devices: the `/dev/ttyACM0` device is only accessible after the system has booted up completely, as it is a virtual device, while the serial console device is always available, right from the system boot till shut down, as it is a real device.

# Basic system management

Now it's time to take a quick tour of some basic system management commands, which may be useful in the next sections.

 Note that the following commands may be used in both the serial console or the SSH terminal emulator.

# File manipulation tools and friends

One of the main principles of Unix systems is that everything is a file. This means that in a Unix system, (almost) everything can be accessed as a file. So, we can use the same commands to read/write a file for every peripheral connected to the system (for example, disks, terminals, serial ports, and so on).

Since this book's main goal is to show you how to get access to the system's peripherals, it's quite obvious that these commands are very important to know. Moreover, in the next chapters, we are going to use several command-line tools to set up our BeagleBone Black and its attached peripherals, so in this section, I'm going to list some of them.

> The following tutorial will not cover all the possible file manipulation and tool commands nor all the possible usages, so let me encourage you to get more information by surfing the Internet. A good starting point is at http://en.wikipedia.org/wiki/List_of_Unix_commands.

Well, in order to manipulate the files, the first commands that we can use are: echo and cat, the former to insert some text into a file and the latter to read the file content:

```
root@BeagleBone:~# echo 'Some text' > /tmp/foo
root@BeagleBone:~# cat /tmp/foo
Some text
```

Note that to append some text, instead of rewriting it, we can simply replace the > char with >> in the preceding command, as shown in the following command:

```
root@BeagleBone:~# echo 'Another line' >> /tmp/foo
root@BeagleBone:~# cat /tmp/foo
Some text
Another line
```

Another useful command is grep that can be used to select some text from a file as follows:

```
root@BeagleBone:~# grep "Another" /tmp/foo
Another line
```

The output is just the line where the word Another is written.

The tail command has already been used before, and there is nothing more to add; however, you will notice that if it is not used with the -f option, the command is simply used to get to the end of an unchanged file.

Another interesting command is od that can be used to inspect a file's contents one byte at time (or in a more complex form). For instance, we can read the preceding /tmp/foo text file one byte at time using a binary format:

```
root@BeagleBone:~# od -tx1 < /tmp/foo
0000000 53 6f 6d 65 20 74 65 78 74 0a 41 6e 6f 74 68 65
```

```
0000020 72 20 6c 69 6e 65 0a
0000027
```

You can easily note that each byte is the ASCII coding of each letter of the preceding strings.

To download a file from a remote system through the HTTP protocol, we can use the wget command in the following form:

```
root@BeagleBone:~# wget http://www.cosino.io/wp-content/uploads/2014/06/
IMG_20140822_135252.jpg
```

Here the argument is just the URL of the file.

The file command is used to detect a file type:

```
root@beaglebone:~# file /tmp/foo
/tmp/foo: ASCII text
root@beaglebone:~# file /dev/urandom
/dev/urandom: character special
root@beaglebone:~# file /usr/bin/file
/usr/bin/file: ELF 32-bit LSB executable, ARM, version 1 (SYSV),
dynamically linked (uses shared libs), for GNU/Linux 2.6.26, BuildID[sha1
]=0x1a5b7b6bc983839b7be5c94bc2049a7f8147fb26, stripped
```

If we take a look at the preceding output, we will discover that the /tmp/foo file we created in the previous examples is just an ASCII text file; the /dev/urandom file is a special character file (we'll see these files in detail in *Chapter 5, Device Drivers*), and /usr/bin/file (that is, where the file command is stored) is an executable file for the ARM platform.

The strings command is used to find strings in a binary file, for example, we can extract the usage string of the file command using the following command:

```
root@beaglebone:~# strings /usr/bin/file | grep Usage
Usage: %s [-bchikLlNnprsvz0] [--apple] [--mime-encoding] [--mime-type]
Usage: file [OPTION...] [FILE...]
```

In any case, you can take all the information regarding a command using the man command as follows:

```
root@beaglebone:~# man <command>
```

Here, <command> is just the name of the command to inspect.

# Package management

In the first chapter, I showed you how install a package in a Debian or Ubuntu compatible distribution; however, there are a few more things to add in order to manage the system's packages.

For example, we know that the installation of the **vim** (**Vi IMproved**) package can be done simply by using the following command:

```
root@BeagleBone:~# aptitude install vim
```

Here, I am assuming that the package containing the vim package has the same name as that of the software tool. However, this is not always true!

For instance, if we wish to install the PHP command-line interface (the tool used to execute the PHP scripts from the command line), we may assume that the package's name was php-cli, and then we can try to install the package using the following command:

```
root@BeagleBone:~# aptitude install php-cli
```

In this case, we will get the following error message:

```
Couldn't find any package whose name or description matched "php-cli"
```

Oh! So, what is the correct package's name? Here is where the apt-cache command comes in handy. Just type the following command on the console:

```
root@BeagleBone:~# apt-cache search php cli
```

We will get a long list of packages related to the php and cli words (in fact, we can assume that both these words may be in both the package's name and description). Now we can search which package suits our needs, and we can try to filter the output using the grep command, as shown in the following command:

```
root@BeagleBone:~# apt-cache search php cli | grep 'php.*cli'
dynalogin-client-php - two-factor HOTP authentication - PHP client
php-cas - Central Authentication Service client library in php
php-xml-rpc2 - PHP XML-RPC client/server library
php5-cli - command-line interpreter for the php5 scripting language
```

> The php.*cli string is a regular expression which asks grep to select
> only those lines that hold a string, which starts with php and ends with
> the cli chars. No matter what is in the middle.
>
> Again, you may get more information on the Internet, and a good starting
> point would be at http://en.wikipedia.org/wiki/Grep.

Now, as we can see, the output is shorter, and after a quick glance, we can notice that
the desired package is named php5-cli.

Another useful command is the apt-file command, which can be used to find
a package that holds a specific file even if it is not installed on the system.

Unfortunately, this command is not installed by default in the BeagleBone Black's
default distribution, so we must install it ourselves:

```
root@BeagleBone:~# aptitude install apt-file
```

When the installation ends, we must update the apt-file data using the
following command:

```
root@BeagleBone:~# apt-file update
```

Now, for example, if we get an error during a compilation, where a file (say,
libcurses.so) is missing, we can obtain package's name that holds the file
using the apt-file command as follows:

```
root@BeagleBone:~# apt-file search libncurses.so
libncurses-gst: /usr/lib/gnu-smalltalk/libncurses.so
libncurses5: /lib/arm-linux-gnueabihf/libncurses.so.5
libncurses5: /lib/arm-linux-gnueabihf/libncurses.so.5.9
libncurses5-dbg: /usr/lib/debug/lib/arm-linux-gnueabihf/libncurses.so.5.9
libncurses5-dbg: /usr/lib/debug/libncurses.so.5
libncurses5-dbg: /usr/lib/debug/libncurses.so.5.9
libncurses5-dev: /usr/lib/arm-linux-gnueabihf/libncurses.so
```

The preceding message shows us that the desired package's name is
libncurses5-dev.

# Managing the kernel messages

As stated before, the serial console is very helpful if we need to see the kernel messages. Now, to see these messages, we can use a terminal emulator through a normal SSH connection by executing the following command:

```
root@BeagleBone:~# tail -f /var/log/kern.log
```

Yes, this is true, but you should consider the following:

- If the system is not yet fully functional, we have *no* network devices to use for the SSH connection.

- Also, using the `tail` command, we may miss the important kernel messages, for example, an **oops** message, where the system can become unstable due to some kernel bugs. In this situation, we need to display the errors as soon as they arrive, and the `tail` command cannot do it safely.

> An **oops** message is an error, a deviation from the correct behavior of the kernel, that produces a kernel panic condition, which may allow the continued operation but with compromised reliability.
>
> The output produced by these errors are typically called Oops messages. They are special kernel debugging messages, which may arrive, for instance, when an interrupt handler causes a system crash, and in this special situation, the `tail` command will not work as expected. Only, the serial console can help the developer.

On the other hand, if we are connected to the serial console, we can capture these special messages since they are displayed on the serial console as soon as they arrive.

Note that if this behavior can be disabled by default, then an easier way to enable it again is using a special file in the `procfs` filesystem named `/proc/sys/kernel/printk`.

If we try to read its content, we get the following output:

```
root@BeagleBone:~# cat /proc/sys/kernel/printk
4       4       1       7
```

These obscure numbers have a well-defined meaning, in particular, the first one represents the error messages level, which will be shown on the serial console.

Let me explain this in a better way. The kernel messages are defined in the `linux/include/linux/kern_levels.h` file.

The **procfs (proc filesystem)** is one of the most important filesystems we can find in a Linux-based system, so you may wish to spend some time to study it. A good starting point can be at http://en.wikipedia.org/wiki/Procfs.

This preceding file is present in Linux's source tree, and in the next chapter, we'll see how to obtain it.

The definitions are as follows:

```
#define KERN_EMERG      KERN_SOH "0"    /* system is unusable */

#define KERN_ALERT      KERN_SOH "1"    /* action must be taken immediately */

#define KERN_CRIT       KERN_SOH "2"    /* critical conditions */

#define KERN_ERR        KERN_SOH "3"    /* error conditions */

#define KERN_WARNING    KERN_SOH "4"    /* warning conditions */

#define KERN_NOTICE     KERN_SOH "5"    /* normal but significant condition */

#define KERN_INFO       KERN_SOH "6"    /* informational */

#define KERN_DEBUG      KERN_SOH "7"    /* debug-level messages */
```

Since the first number in the /proc/sys/kernel/printk file is 4, this means that the only messages displayed will be KERN_EMERG, KERN_ALERT, KERN_CRIT, and KERN_ERR.

Now it's quite simple to guess whether to enable all the kernel messages. To do this, we must replace the first number 4 with 8, because there are no kernel messages with a lower priority than 7:

```
root@BeagleBone:~# echo 8 > /proc/sys/kernel/printk
```

Note that the kernel messages' priorities start from 0 (high priority) and go up to 7 (low priority).

On the other hand, we can disable all the kernel messages using the number 0:

```
root@BeagleBone:~# echo 0 > /proc/sys/kernel/printk
```

Note that the preceding commands just replace the first number; in fact, if we read the file content again, we get the output as follows:

```
root@BeagleBone:~# cat /proc/sys/kernel/printk
0       4       1       7
```

# A quick tour of the bootloader

As stated, at the beginning of this chapter, using the serial console, we can get access to the bootloader.

Actually, the BeagleBone Black has two bootloaders: one named SPL, which is the prebootloader that initializes the hardware components, such as the RAM and some mass storage devices, and the second named U-Boot, which is the real bootloader that initializes almost all the peripherals and has support for, among other things, booting over a network, and a scriptable shell through which basic commands can be given. Now the one million dollar question is: why should a developer be able to manage the bootloader too?

Well, the answers are more than one, however, the most important are as follows:

- By passing a well-formed command line to the kernel, we can change some functionalities in the running filesystem.
- From the bootloader, we can easily manage a **factory restore** method (this is usually made with a hidden button in a tiny hole on the system's box. By keeping this button pressed while powering up the system, the user can cause the whole system to reset to its factory defaults).
- Using the bootloader, we can decide which device to use to perform a boot. For instance, we can force a boot from a microSD or from a USB key.

So, now let's see how we can get the U-Boot's prompt.

Just after the power up, we will see some interesting messages on the serial console:

```
U-Boot SPL 2014.04-00014-g47880f5 (Apr 22 2014 - 13:23:54)
reading args
spl_load_image_fat_os: error reading image args, err - -1
reading u-boot.img
reading u-boot.img

...

cpsw, usb_ether
Hit any key to stop autoboot:  1
```

At this time, we have less than 3 seconds to strike the *Enter* key to stop the countdown and get the U-Boot's prompt. So, if we are quick enough to hit *Enter*, we'll get the following prompt:

```
U-Boot#
```

Well, now we can get a list of available commands using the `help` command:

```
U-Boot# help
?         - alias for 'help'
askenv    - get environment variables from stdin
base      - print or set address offset
bdinfo    - print Board Info structure
boot      - boot default, i.e., run 'bootcmd'
bootd     - boot default, i.e., run 'bootcmd'
...
usb       - USB sub-system
usbboot - boot from USB device
version - print monitor, compiler and linker version
```

As we can see, the list is quite long, however, due to spacing reasons, I cannot report or explain all the commands, so we'll take a look at the most important ones.

 For more information regarding the U-Boot bootloader, you may take a look at the user manual at http://www.denx. de/wiki/DULG/Manual.

# GPIOs management

The first (and the simplest) command I'd like to show you is the `gpio` command that can be used to control the user LEDs, as for the others, the GPIOs lines of the BeagleBone Black.

The **GPIO (General Purpose Input Output)** signals are input/output pins with no special purpose defined; when a developer needs one of them to work as an input pin or as an output pin (or another function), he/she can easily reconfigure the CPU in order to accommodate his/her needs.

If we take a look at the output of the `help` command, we should get something like this:

```
U-Boot# help gpio
gpio - query and control gpio pins

Usage:
```

```
gpio <input|set|clear|toggle> <pin>
    - input/set/clear/toggle the specified pin
gpio status [<bank> | <pin>]
```

On our BeagleBone Black, the LEDs are mapped as follows:

| Name | GPIO |
|------|------|
| USR0 | 53 |
| USR1 | 54 |
| USR2 | 55 |
| USR3 | 56 |

So, we can easily deduce that to toggle the USR0 LED, we can use the following commands:

```
U-Boot# gpio toggle 53
gpio: pin 53 (gpio 53) value is 1
U-Boot# gpio toggle 53
gpio: pin 53 (gpio 53) value is 0
```

Of course, we can turn the LED on and off, simply, using the set and clear options respectively, while the input option can be used to read the input status of the related GPIO line.

You can take a look at what these LEDs are used for at http://beagleboard.org/getting-started.

# The environment

One of the most important features of U-Boot is the environment. We can store whatever we need to accomplish a safe system boot in the environment. We can store variables, commands, and even complete scripts in it.

To check the environment content, we can use the print command:

```
U-Boot# print
arch=arm
baudrate=115200
board=am335x
board_name=A335BNLT
```

```
board_rev=00C0
boot_fdt=try
...
stdout=serial
usbnet_devaddr=78:a5:04:ca:cb:00
vendor=ti
ver=U-Boot 2014.04-00014-g47880f5 (Apr 22 2014 - 13:23:54)

Environment size: 4725/131068 bytes
```

As for the commands stored in the environment, the list is quite long too, and we will find a lot of interesting information in it. If we need to inspect a specific variable, we can use the print command:

```
U-Boot# print loadaddr
loadaddr=0x82000000
```

 loadaddr is a memory address mapped into the system's RAM, where we can store the temporary information.

We can also inspect a complete script using the print command again:

```
U-Boot# print bootcmd
bootcmd=gpio set 53; i2c mw 0x24 1 0x3e; run findfdt; run mmcboot;gpio
clear 56; gpio clear 55; gpio clear 54; setenv mmcdev 1; setenv bootpart
1:1; run mmcboot; run nandboot;
```

 The bootcmd command is the default boot command, which is executed each time the system starts.

The command output is quite cryptic; due to the fact that the newline (\n) characters are missing (although, U-Boot doesn't need them to correctly interpret a script); however, to make the output more readable, I have rewritten the preceding output with the necessary newline characters:

```
gpio set 53; \n
i2c mw 0x24 1 0x3e; \n
run findfdt; \n
run mmcboot; \n
gpio clear 56; \n
```

```
gpio clear 55; \n
gpio clear 54; \n
setenv mmcdev 1; \n
setenv bootpart 1:1; \n
run mmcboot; \n
run nandboot;
```

To write/modify an environment's variable, we can use the `setenv` command:

```
U-Boot# setenv myvar 12345
U-Boot# print myvar
myvar=12345
```

We can read the variable content by prefixing its name with the $ character:

```
U-Boot# echo "myvar is set to: $myvar"
myvar is set to: 12345
```

In a similar manner, we can use the following command to write a script:

```
U-Boot# setenv myscript 'while sleep 1 ; do gpio toggle 53 ; done'
```

 Note that I have used the two ticks to delimitate the script commands!

Again, here, I did not add the newlines; however, this time, the script is quite simple and readable. In fact, with the newline characters, the output should appear as follows:

```
while sleep 1 ; do
        gpio toggle 53 ;
done
```

In the end, we can run a script using the `run` command as follows:

```
U-Boot# run myscript
gpio: pin 53 (gpio 53) value is 1
gpio: pin 53 (gpio 53) value is 0
gpio: pin 53 (gpio 53) value is 1
gpio: pin 53 (gpio 53) value is 0
...
```

If we write the command correctly now, the USR0 LED should blink at a frequency of 1 Hz.

 We can stop the script by hitting the *Ctrl + C* keys.

Note that the environment is reset each time the system starts, but it can be altered by modifying the environment file in the microSD (see the next section).

In case, we make some errors, don't panic! We can edit the variable with the following command:

```
U-Boot# env edit myscript
edit: while sleep 1 ; do gpio toggle 53 ; done
```

Now, we can do all the needed modifications to the script in an easy manner.

# Managing the storage devices

We already know that the BeagleBone Black's on-board mass storage is based on **MMC (Multi Media Card)** support, this means that the system can boot from the on-board eMMC or (as in the *(Re)Installing Debian* section of *Chapter 1, Installing the Developing System*) from a preconfigured microSD, so it's very important to know how we can manage a MMC device within the bootloader.

MMC support is implemented with the mmcinfo and mmc commands. The former can be used to get some useful information about the microSD/MMC present on the selected MMC slot, while the latter can be used to effectively manage the microSD.

Let's take a look at some examples.

We know that our BeagleBone Black has an on-board eMMC on MMC slot 1, so to get some information about this device, firstly, we should select the MMC slot to examine using following command:

```
U-Boot# mmc dev 1
mmc1(part 0) is current device
```

Then, we can ask for the MMC device's information using the mmcinfo command:

```
U-Boot# mmcinfo
Device: OMAP SD/MMC
Manufacturer ID: 70
```

```
OEM: 100
Name: MMC04
Tran Speed: 52000000
Rd Block Len: 512
MMC version 4.5
High Capacity: Yes
Capacity: 3.6 GiB
Bus Width: 4-bit
```

In the same manner, we can examine the alternate-booting microSD we built earlier (see *Chapter 1, Installing the Developing System*). Just insert this into the microSD slot, and then use the preceding commands to inspect it. Here is the output that appears on my system:

```
U-Boot# mmc dev 0
mmc0(part 0) is current device
U-Boot# mmcinfo
Device: OMAP SD/MMC
Manufacturer ID: 41
OEM: 3432
Name: SD4GB
Tran Speed: 50000000
Rd Block Len: 512
SD version 3.0
High Capacity: Yes
Capacity: 3.7 GiB
Bus Width: 4-bit
```

Now we can examine the microSD partition table using the following command:

```
U-Boot# mmc part
```

```
Partition Map for MMC device 0  --  Partition Type: DOS
```

| Part | Start Sector | Num Sectors | UUID | Type |
|------|--------------|-------------|------|------|
| 1 | 2048 | 24576 | 00000000-01 | 0e Boot |
| 2 | 26624 | 7747584 | 00000000-02 | 83 |

The first partition is the /boot directory (that is, the directory where the boot files are placed in the root filesystem) while the second partition is the system's root filesystem. Let's examine the /boot directory:

```
U-Boot# fatls mmc 0:1
    70596   mlo
   374548   u-boot.img
      681   bbb-uenv.txt
      667   nfs-uenv.txt

4 file(s), 0 dir(s)
```

We found the prebootloader image (the mlo file), the bootloader itself (the u-boot. img file), and some environment files that U-Boot can load during the boot (the bbb-uenv.txt and nfs-uenv.txt files).

Now, for example, to import the bbb-uenv.txt file content, we can use the load command:

```
U-Boot# load mmc 0:1 $loadaddr bbb-uenv.txt
reading bbb-uenv.txt
681 bytes read in 5 ms (132.8 KiB/s)
```

This command loads a file from the microSD into the RAM, then we can parse it, and store the data in the environment using the env command:

```
U-Boot# env import -t $loadaddr $filesize
```

To save a variable/command in the environment (in such a way that the new value is reloaded at the next boot), we can use U-Boot itself, but the procedure is quite complex and, in my humble opinion, the quickest and simplest way to do it is to just put the microSD on a host PC and then change the file on it.

# The kernel command line

Now, it's time to take a look at the way U-Boot uses a command line to pass to the kernel. This data is very important because it can be used to configure the kernel and to pass some instructions to the user's programs in the root filesystem.

These arguments are stored in the bootargs variable, but if we stop the BeagleBone Black's bootloader, as shown earlier, we can see that this variable is not set at all:

```
U-Boot# print bootargs
## Error: "bootargs" not defined
```

This is because its content is set up by the booting scripts that are not executed if we stop the boot. On our system, by carefully reading the U-Boot environment, we can discover that, before or after, the `run mmcargs` command is called. This command is written as follows:

```
U-Boot# print mmcargs
mmcargs=setenv bootargs console=${console} ${optargs} root=${mmcroot}
rootfstype=${mmcrootfstype}
```

Here is where the kernel command line is built. You can now try to understand which values are used for all the preceding variables; the only thing I wish to add is that we can add our custom settings using the `optargs` variable.

For instance, if we wish to set the `loglevel` kernel (that is the lower kernel message-priority shown on the serial console, as seen in the preceding section, *Managing the kernel messages*), we can set `optargs` to the following:

```
U-Boot# setenv optargs 'loglevel=8'
```

Then, you are asked to continue with the boot:

```
U-Boot# boot
```

Once the system has been restarted, we can verify the new setting by looking into the `procfs` file, which holds a copy of the kernel command line, that is the `/proc/cmdline` file, using the command:

```
root@BeagleBone:~# cat /proc/cmdline
console=tty0 console=ttyO0,115200n8 loglevel=8 root=UUID=4d5e50d8-fda1-
4c02-b2b2-cf7e957864d0 ro rootfstype=ext4 rootwait fixrtc quiet init=/
lib/systemd/systemd
```

> More information regarding the kernel command line and its parameters can be found in the kernel tree in the `Documentation/kernel-parameters.txt` file or online at `https://www.kernel.org/doc/Documentation/kernel-parameters.txt`.

# Summary

In this chapter, we saw how files are manipulated and kernel messages are managed. We also learned about some crucial bootloader commands and microSD management that will help us in the forthcoming chapters. Also, we were familiarized with the operation of the U-Boot bootloader and were able to learn a few commands that can help us if the BeagleBone Black gets stuck while booting.

Now it's time to compile and/or cross-compile programs to get the maximum performance from our embedded system and to be able to fully customize it.

So, let's go to the third chapter.

# 3
# Compiling versus Cross-compiling

Now it's time to play hard! We are going to see how a C compiler works, starting from compiling a simple C program to compiling the whole BeagleBone Black's kernel.

Knowing how to compile a program is useful in order to get the best performance from an embedded computer, and knowing how to compile the kernel is useful in order to be able to use the latest kernel release with the new and updated drivers and features. In this chapter, you will learn all about the compiling steps in both kernel and user-space to easily add a new driver not included in the standard BeagleBone Black's kernel, and/or how to recompile a user-space tool not included in the Debian distribution.

In this chapter, we will also see the difference between a compiler and a cross-compiler, and try to understand when it is better to use either one of them.

## Native compilation versus cross-compilation

Programs for embedded systems based on ARM, MIPS and other non-PC architectures are traditionally written and compiled using a cross-compiler for that architecture on a host PC. This is the reason why we use a compiler that can generate the code for a foreign machine architecture, which means a different CPU instruction set from the compiler host's one.

For example, the BeagleBone Black is an ARM machine while (most probably) our host machine is an x86 PC (that is a normal PC), so if we try to compile a C program on our host machine, the generated code cannot be used on the BeagleBone Black and vice versa.

Let's verify this. Here is the classic *Hello World* program from *The compiler* section of Chapter 1, *Installing the Developing System*. Now we compile this program on our host machine using the following command:

```
$ make CFLAGS="-Wall -O2" helloworld
cc -Wall -O2    helloworld.c   -o helloworld
```

We can verify that this file is for the x86 (that is, the PC) platform using the file command:

```
$ file helloworld
helloworld: ELF 64-bit LSB  executable, x86-64, version 1 (SYSV),
dynamically linked (uses shared libs), for GNU/Linux 2.6.24, BuildID[sha1
]=0f0db5e65e1cd09957ad06a7c1b7771d949dfc84, not stripped
```

> Note that the output may vary according to your host machine's platform.

Now we can just copy the program to the BeagleBone Black and try to execute it:

```
root@BeagleBone:~# ./helloworld
-bash: ./helloworld: cannot execute binary file
```

As expected, the system refuses to execute the code generated for a different architecture.

On the other hand, if we use a cross-compiler for this specific CPU architecture, the program will run like a charm. Let's verify this by recompiling the code, but we need to specify that we wish to use the cross-compiler instead. So, delete the previously generated x86 executable file (just in case) using the `rm helloworld` command and then recompile it using the cross-compiler:

```
$ make CC=arm-linux-gnueabihf-gcc CFLAGS="-Wall -O2" helloworld
arm-linux-gnueabihf-gcc -Wall -O2    helloworld.c   -o helloworld
```

> Note that the cross-compiler's filename has a special meaning: the form is `<architecture>-<platform>-<binary-format>-<tool-name>`. So, the `arm-linux-gnueabihf-gcc` filename means: ARM architecture, Linux platform, **gnueabihf (GNU EABI hard float)** binary format, and **gcc (GNU C Compiler)** tool.

Now we will use the `file` command again to see whether the code is indeed generated for the ARM architecture:

```
$ file helloworld
helloworld: ELF 32-bit LSB  executable, ARM, EABI5 version 1 (SYSV),
dynamically linked (uses shared libs), for GNU/Linux 2.6.32, BuildID[sha1
]=31251570b8a17803b0e0db01fb394a6394de8d2d, not stripped
```

Now if we transfer the file as we did earlier in the BeagleBone Black and try to execute it, we get the following output:

```
root@BeagleBone:~# ./helloworld
Hello World!
```

Therefore, we can see that the cross-compiler ensures that the generated code is compatible with the architecture we are executing it on.

Now the question is: when should I use the compiler and when the cross-compiler?

We should use the compiler on the BeagleBone Black because:

- We can.
- There would be no compatibility issues, as all the target libraries will be available. In cross-compilation, it becomes hell when we need all the libraries (if the project uses any) in the ARM format on the host PC. So, we not only have to cross-compile the program but also its dependencies. However, if the same version dependencies are not installed on the BeagleBone Black's `rootfs`, then good luck with troubleshooting!
- It's easy and quick.

We should use the cross-compiler because:

- We are working on a large code base, and we don't want to waste too much time compiling the program on the BeagleBone Black, which may take from several minutes to several hours. This reason might be strong enough to overpower the other reasons in favor of compiling on the BeagleBone Black itself.
- PCs nowadays have multiple cores, so the compiler can process more files simultaneously.
- We are building a full Linux system from scratch.

In any case, in the next sections, I will show you examples of both native compilation and cross-compilation of a software package so that you may well understand the difference between them.

# Compiling a user-space software package

The first step is to see how we can compile a user-space tool. This could be useful because it may happen that a specific tool is missing in our distribution or we may need to work around package version problems; in these cases, we need to know some basic techniques to work around these problems. To show the difference between a native compilation and a cross-compilation, I will explain both the methods. However, a word of caution for you here, this guide is not exhaustive at all. In fact, the cross-compilation steps may vary according to the software packages we are going to cross-compile.

The package that we are going to use is the PicoC interpreter. All Real Programmers (TM) know the C compiler, which is normally used to translate a C program into machine language, but (maybe) not all of them know that a C interpreter exists too.

Actually, there are many C interpreters, but we will focus our attention on PicoC due its simplicity in cross-compiling it.

As we already know, an interpreter is a program that converts the source code into an executable code on the fly, does not need to parse the complete file, and generates the code at once.

This is quite useful when we need a flexible way to write brief programs to resolve easy tasks. In fact, to fix bugs in the code and/or change the program's behavior, we simply have to change the program source, and then re-execute it without any compilation at all. We just need an editor to change our code.

For instance, if we wish to read some bytes from a file, we can do this using a standard C program, but for this easy task, we can write a script for an interpreter too. Which interpreter to choose is up to the developer, and since I'm a C programmer, the choice is quite obvious. This is the reason I have decided to use PicoC.

Note that the PicoC tool is quite far from being able to interpret all C programs. In fact, this tool implements a fraction of the features of a standard C compiler; however, it can be used for several common and easy tasks. Please consider the PicoC tool as an educational tool and avoid using it in a production environment.

# Native compilation

Well, as a first step, we need to download the PicoC source code from the Google Code repository at `https://code.google.com/p/picoc/`. However, before we download it, we need to install the Subversion tool in our BeagleBone Black. The command is as follows:

```
# aptitude install subversion
```

When finished, we can download the PicoC source code using the following command:

```
# svn checkout http://picoc.googlecode.com/svn/trunk/ picoc-read-only
A    picoc-read-only/expression.c
...
A    picoc-read-only/picoc.c
Checked out revision 608.
```

Ok, now we will go to the newly created `picoc-read-only` directory, and then we will use the `make` command as follows:

```
# cd picoc-read-only/
# make
```

 This software package has a very simple compiling method, just a simple Makefile. However, it is quite easy to find software packages that use more complex and complete compiling methods, such as (the most used) the autotools suite. In this case, the compilation command is as follows:

```
$ ./configure && make
```

However, during the compilation, we get the following output:

```
platform/platform_unix.c:5:31: fatal error: readline/readline.h: No such
file or directory
compilation terminated.
make: *** [platform/platform_unix.o] Error 1
```

Bad news, we have got an error! This is because the `readline` library is missing; so, we need to install it to keep this going. Remember what we discussed in the *Package Management* section of *Chapter 2, Managing the System Console*, in order to discover which package's name holds a specific tool, we can use the following command to discover the package that holds the `readline` library:

```
# apt-cache search readline
```

The command output is quite long, but if we carefully take a look at it, we can see the following lines:

```
libreadline5 - GNU readline and history libraries, run-time libraries
libreadline5-dbg - GNU readline and history libraries, debugging libraries
libreadline-dev - GNU readline and history libraries, development files
libreadline6 - GNU readline and history libraries, run-time libraries
libreadline6-dbg - GNU readline and history libraries, debugging libraries
libreadline6-dev - GNU readline and history libraries, development files
```

This is exactly what we need to know. The required package is named `libreadline-dev`.

In the Debian distribution, all the library's packages are prefixed with the `lib` string, while the `-dev` postfix is used to mark the development version of a library package. Also, note that I chose the `libreadline-dev` package intentionally, leaving the system to choose to install Version 5 or 6 of the library.

The development version of a library package holds all the needed files that allow the developer to compile his/her software with the library itself and/or some documentation about the library's functions.

For instance, in the development version of the `readline` library package (that is, in the `libreadline6-dev` package), we can find the header and the object files needed by the compiler. We can see these files using the following command:

```
# dpkg -L libreadline6-dev | egrep '\.(so|h)'
/usr/include/readline/rltypedefs.h
/usr/include/readline/readline.h
/usr/include/readline/history.h
/usr/include/readline/keymaps.h
/usr/include/readline/rlconf.h
/usr/include/readline/tilde.h
/usr/include/readline/rlstdc.h
/usr/include/readline/chardefs.h
/usr/lib/arm-linux-gnueabihf/libreadline.so
/usr/lib/arm-linux-gnueabihf/libhistory.so
```

So, let's install it:

```
# aptitude install libreadline-dev
```

When finished, we can relaunch the `make` command to definitely compile our new C interpreter:

```
# make
gcc -Wall -pedantic -g -DUNIX_HOST -DVER=\"`svnversion -n`\"   -c -o
clibrary.o clibrary.c

...

gcc -Wall -pedantic -g -DUNIX_HOST -DVER=\"`svnversion -n`\" -o picoc
picoc.o table.o lex.o parse.o expression.o heap.o type.o variable.o
clibrary.o platform.o include.o debug.o platform/platform_unix.o
platform/library_unix.o cstdlib/stdio.o cstdlib/math.o cstdlib/string.o
cstdlib/stdlib.o cstdlib/time.o cstdlib/errno.o cstdlib/ctype.o cstdlib/
stdbool.o cstdlib/unistd.o -lm -lreadline
```

Well, now the tool is successfully compiled as expected.

To test it, we can again use the standard *Hello World* program from *The compiler* section of *Chapter 1, Installing the Developing System*, but with a little modification, in fact, the `main()` function is not defined as before. This is because PicoC returns an error if we use the typical function definition. Here is the code:

```
#include <stdio.h>

int main()
{
        printf("Hello World\n");

        return 0;
}
```

Now we can directly execute it (that is, without compiling it) using our new C interpreter:

```
# ./picoc helloworld.c
Hello World
```

An interesting feature of PicoC is that it can execute a C source file, such as a script, that is, we don't need to specify a `main()` function as C requires, and the instructions are executed one by one from the beginning of the file, as a normal scripting language does.

Just to show this, we can use the following script, which implements the *Hello World* program as a C-like script (note that the `main()` function is not defined):

```
printf("Hello World!\n");
return 0;
```

If we insert the preceding code into the `helloworld.picoc` file, we can execute it using the following command:

```
# ./picoc -s helloworld.picoc
Hello World!
```

Note that this time, we will add the `-s` option argument to the command line in order to instruct the PicoC interpreter to use its scripting behavior.

# Cross-compilation

Now let's try to cross-compile PicoC interpreter on the host system. As we did earlier, we need to download the PicoC's source code using the same `svn` command as earlier. Now we have to enter the following command in the newly created `picoc-read-only` directory:

```
$ cd picoc-read-only/
$ make CC=arm-linux-gnueabihf-gcc
arm-linux-gnueabihf-gcc -Wall -pedantic -g -DUNIX_HOST
-DVER=\"`svnversion -n`\"    -c -o picoc.o picoc.c
...

arm-linux-gnueabihf-gcc -Wall -pedantic -g -DUNIX_HOST
-DVER=\"`svnversion -n`\" -o picoc picoc.o table.o lex.o parse.o
expression.o heap.o type.o variable.o clibrary.o platform.o include.o
debug.o platform/platform_unix.o platform/library_unix.o cstdlib/stdio.o
cstdlib/math.o cstdlib/string.o cstdlib/stdlib.o cstdlib/time.o cstdlib/
errno.o cstdlib/ctype.o cstdlib/stdbool.o cstdlib/unistd.o -lm -lreadline
/usr/lib/gcc-cross/arm-linux-gnueabihf/4.7/../../../../arm-linux-
gnueabihf/bin/ld: cannot find -lreadline
collect2: error: ld returned 1 exit status
make: *** [picoc] Error 1
```

 Note that we will specify the `CC=arm-linux-gnueabihf-gcc` command line option to force the cross-compilation. However, as already stated before, the cross-compilation commands may vary according to the compilation method used by the single software package.

As before, the system returns a linking error because the `readline` library is missing; however, this time, we cannot install it, as before, since we need the ARM version (specifically, the **armhf** version) of this library, and my host system is a normal PC.

Actually, there is a way to install a foreign package in a Debian/Ubuntu distribution, but it's not a simple task nor it's within the scope of this book. You may take a look at the Debian/Ubuntu Multiarch at `https://help.ubuntu.com/community/MultiArch`.

Now we have to resolve this issue and we have two possibilities:

- We can try to find a way to install the missing package
- We can try to find a way to continue the compilation without it

The former method is quite complex since the `readline` library has, in turn, other dependencies, and we may take a lot of time trying to compile them all, so let's try to use the latter option.

Knowing that the `readline` library is just used to implement powerful interactive tools (such as recalling a previous command line to re-edit it, and so on.), and since we are not interested in the interactive usage of this interpreter, we can hope to avoid using it. So, if we carefully take a look at the code, we can see that `define USE_READLINE` exists and changing the code, as shown in the following code, should resolve the issue, allowing us to compile the tool without the `readline` support:

```
$ svn diff
Index: Makefile
===================================================================
--- Makefile (revision 608)
+++ Makefile (working copy)
@@ -1,6 +1,6 @@
 CC=gcc
 CFLAGS=-Wall -pedantic -g -DUNIX_HOST -DVER=\"`svnversion -n`\"
-LIBS=-lm -lreadline
+LIBS=-lm

 TARGET= picoc
 SRCS= picoc.c table.c lex.c parse.c expression.c heap.c type.c \
Index: platform.h
===================================================================
```

```
--- platform.h        (revision 608)
+++ platform.h        (working copy)
@@ -49,7 +49,7 @@
 # ifndef NO_FP
 #   include <math.h>
 #   define PICOC_MATH_LIBRARY
-#   define USE_READLINE
+/* #   define USE_READLINE */
 #   undef BIG_ENDIAN
 #   if defined(__powerpc__) || defined(__hppa__) || defined(__sparc__)
 #     define BIG_ENDIAN
```

 Each revision control system has its own proper command to show the developer the changes to be applied to the code, and most of them are based on (or derived from) the diff command that, as already stated, can use the *unified context diff* format.

The preceding output is in the unified context diff format, and let me remind you what it means. Lines starting with the + character must be added while the ones starting with a – character must be removed from the indexed file; so, the preceding code specifies that in the Makefile file, the -lreadline option must be removed from the LIBS variable, and then in the platform.h file, the USE_READLINE define must be commented out.

After all the changes are in place, we can try to recompile the package with the same command as before:

```
$ make CC=arm-linux-gnueabihf-gcc
arm-linux-gnueabihf-gcc -Wall -pedantic -g -DUNIX_HOST
-DVER=\"`svnversion -n`\"    -c -o table.o table.c
...

arm-linux-gnueabihf-gcc -Wall -pedantic -g -DUNIX_HOST
-DVER=\"`svnversion -n`\" -o picoc picoc.o table.o lex.o parse.o
expression.o heap.o type.o variable.o clibrary.o platform.o include.o
debug.o platform/platform_unix.o platform/library_unix.o cstdlib/stdio.o
cstdlib/math.o cstdlib/string.o cstdlib/stdlib.o cstdlib/time.o cstdlib/
errno.o cstdlib/ctype.o cstdlib/stdbool.o cstdlib/unistd.o -lm
```

Great! We did it! Now, just to verify that everything is working correctly, we can simply copy the picoc file to our BeagleBone Black and test it as before.

# Compiling the kernel

In the previous section, we first saw the difference between the native compilation and cross-compilation of a user-space program. In the preceding example, it's quite obvious that the native compilation wins, but as already stated, there are some circumstances where the cross-compilation is a must.

One of these cases is the kernel compilation.

In the older days of embedded programming, when the embedded systems were really small in the sense of limited resources (from 4 MB to 32 MB of RAM memory and 32 MB to 128 MB mass storage memory), recompiling the kernel natively was considered foolish. However, day by day and year by year, the embedded systems became more powerful, and now we have 1 GB or 2 GB of RAM memory and 4 GB to 32 GB of mass storage, which makes it easier to recompile, even if its not much of a common practice. So, nowadays, considering recompiling the whole kernel can be possible, but we've to take into account that compiling the BeagleBone Black's kernel natively may take several hours, but the same job can be done within 10 minutes on a reasonably fast host PC.

So, even if the kernel native compilation is simpler than cross-compilation, the latter is still the best solution.

# The Linux kernel

Even if the kernel compilation steps are quite standard, each embedded system has its own tools and intricacies that need to be taken care of, and the BeagleBone Black has several. However, in this book, I'm going to present a good and easy solution that can be used by novice developers too.

Before we start with the required steps, we must focus our attention on the reasons why a developer may wish to recompile the kernel. The reasons are several but the most important ones are as follows:

- A newer kernel version is required. It may happen that our current kernel version is quite old, and it misses one or more features (or drivers) that a newer kernel implements instead. In this case, updating the kernel is more easy than doing a backport of the desired features (even if the kernel recompilation must be done in both the cases).

- The current kernel has one or more severe bugs. Our kernel may work correctly for months, but as soon as a bug arrives, the whole system becomes unusable. This is why a bug fix in the kernel and the consequent recompilation is very important for the overall health of our kernel.

For example, we can consider adding the hardware random number generator support to our BeagleBone Black, which is missing in our current kernel (my BeagleBone Black currently runs on the kernel Version 3.8.13), but the random number generator support has been introduced in Version 3.13.

The first step is to download the kernel sources using the following command:

```
$ git clone git://git.kernel.org/pub/scm/linux/kernel/git/torvalds/linux.
git linux-stable
```

 You can skip this step if he/she already has a `git` kernel archive.

Now, we have to download the compilation suite that we are going to use to recompile the kernel:

```
$ git clone git://github.com/RobertCNelson/linux-dev.git
```

When finished, we must enter to the `linux-dev` directory and then check out the kernel Version 3.13:

```
$ git checkout am33x-v3.13
Branch am33x-v3.13 set up to track remote branch am33x-v3.13 from origin.
Switched to a new branch 'am33x-v3.13'
```

Now we should configure the compilation suite by generating a proper configuration file named `system.sh`:

```
$ cp system.sh.sample system.sh
```

On my system, I modified the new `system.sh` file with the following settings:

```
CC=/usr/bin/arm-linux-gnueabihf-
```

The cross-compiler is the one we used before, but note that I used the cross-compiler's prefix, not the filename:

```
LINUX_GIT=/home/giometti/Projects/packt/beagleboneblack/kernel/linux-
stable
```

By setting this variable, I can tell the compilation suite that I already have a kernel repository. This step is not required, but since I have already downloaded the kernel sources, this can save my time:

```
MMC=/dev/sdd
```

This variable is used by the installer tool (named `install_kernel.sh`), and it points to the device corresponding to the microSD, where the BeagleBone system is installed.

> Pay attention to the fact that to test for updating the kernel, I decided to use the microSD we built in the *(Re)Installing Debian* section of *Chapter 1, Installing the Developing System*, and not the on-board eMMC. This is just a precaution in case something goes wrong. In fact, if the new kernel hangs, we can recover the system by just removing the offending microSD.

After all the modifications are in place, using the `diff` command, we should get the following differences:

```
$ diff -u system.sh.sample system.sh
--- system.sh.sample    2014-11-07 21:36:43.543396105 +0100
+++ system.sh   2014-11-09 19:38:31.440735410 +0100
@@ -15,13 +15,13 @@
 #if CC is not set, a known working linaro based gcc compiler will be
downloaded and utilized.
 #CC=<enter full path>/bin/arm-none-eabi-
 #CC=<enter full path>/bin/arm-linux-gnueabi-
-#CC=<enter full path>/bin/arm-linux-gnueabihf-
+CC=/usr/bin/arm-linux-gnueabihf-


 ###OPTIONAL:


 ###OPTIONAL: LINUX_GIT: specify location of locally cloned git tree.
 #
-#LINUX_GIT=/home/user/linux-stable/
+LINUX_GIT=/home/giometti/Projects/packt/beagleboneblack/kernel/linux-
stable


 ###OPTIONAL: GIT_OVER_HTTP: clone over http vs git: git clone http://
 #
@@ -60,7 +60,7 @@
 #WRONG: MMC=/dev/sde1
 #CORRECT: MMC=/dev/sde
 #
```

```
-#MMC=/dev/sde
+MMC=/dev/sdd
```

###ADVANCED:

Warning! You must pay attention and be sure about the MMC define settings or the host machine may get damaged. See the *(Re)Installing Debian* section of *Chapter 1, Installing the Developing System,* for further information on how to choose the right device.

Ok, now we are ready to start our first kernel recompilation. Just run the following command, and the host machine will start the compiling procedure:

```
$ ./build_kernel.sh
```

This step and the subsequent one are time consuming and require patience, so you should take a cup of your preferred tea or coffee and just wait.

After some time, the procedure will present the standard kernel configuration panel, as shown in the following screenshot:

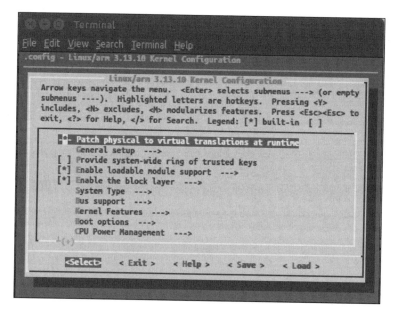

In order to add the hardware random number generator support, as requested earlier, we must enable the kernel configuration settings:

```
<*> Device Drivers > Character devices > TPM HW Random Number Generator
Support
<*> Device Drivers > Character devices > TPM Hardware Support
<*> Device Drivers > Character devices > TPM Hardware Support > TPM
Interface Specification 1.2 Interface (I2C - Atmel)
```

The preceding syntax tells you that you must select the menu item, **Device Drivers**, then **Character devices**, and so on. Also, note that all the settings must be enabled as kernel built-in (**<\*>**) and not as kernel modules (**<M>**). See the following screenshot:

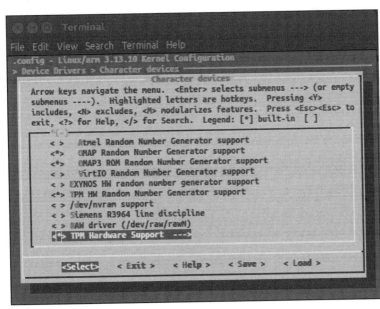

After finishing with the new settings, just save the new kernel configuration and leave the procedure to continue. Then, when it ends, the new kernel image is ready, and we can install it on the microSD using the installation tool:

```
$ ./tools/install_kernel.sh
```

 Note that if the command is executed by an unprivileged user, the script will ask for the root's password.

Before updating the kernel, the tool asks whether the user is really sure about the correct device where the kernel must be placed. On my system, I get the following output:

```
I see...
fdisk -l:
Disk /dev/sda: 500.1 GB, 500107862016 bytes
Disk /dev/sdc: 1000.2 GB, 1000204883968 bytes
Disk /dev/sdb: 1000.2 GB, 1000204883968 bytes
Disk /dev/md0: 1000.1 GB, 1000066842624 bytes
Disk /dev/sdd: 3980 MB, 3980394496 bytes

lsblk:
NAME        MAJ:MIN RM    SIZE RO TYPE  MOUNTPOINT
sda          8:0     0  465.8G  0 disk
|-sda1       8:1     0   21.5G  0 part
|-sda2       8:2     0  116.4G  0 part
|-sda3       8:3     0      1K  0 part
`-sda5       8:5     0  327.9G  0 part  /
sdb          8:16    0  931.5G  0 disk
`-sdb1       8:17    0  931.5G  0 part
  `-md0      9:0     0  931.4G  0 raid1 /media/giometti/DataDisk
sdc          8:32    0  931.5G  0 disk
`-sdc1       8:33    0  931.5G  0 part
  `-md0      9:0     0  931.4G  0 raid1 /media/giometti/DataDisk
sdd          8:48    1    3.7G  0 disk
|-sdd1       8:49    1    12M   0 part  /media/giometti/BOOT
`-sdd2       8:50    1    3.7G  0 part  /media/giometti/rootfs
----------------------------
Are you 100% sure, on selecting [/dev/sdd] (y/n)?
```

My MMC variable is set to /dev/sdd, so if I carefully take a look at the corresponding lines, I can verify that these are the right names of the BeagleBone Black's filesystem, so I can safely answer yes by entering the *y* char.

At the end of the command execution, we should get the output as follows:

```
This script has finished...
For verification, always test this media with your end device...
```

Now just remove the microSD from the host machine, and put it on the BeagleBone Black, and turn it on by keeping the user button pressed in order to force the boot from the microSD (see the figure in the *A*

section *Chapter 1, Installing the Developing System*, to see where the button is placed). If everything works well on the serial console, we should see the standard booting sequence, and after the login, we can verify that the new kernel is really running using the following command:

```
# uname -a
Linux arm 3.13.10-bone9 #1 SMP Fri Nov 7 23:25:59 CET 2014 armv7l GNU/
Linux
```

Ok, everything works well! However, remember that we decided to compile the kernel in order to add the hardware random numbers generator support, so let's see if it's working too.

This new peripheral should be now available at the /dev/hwrng device:

```
# ls -l /dev/hwrng
crw------- 1 root root 10, 183 Jan  1  1970 /dev/hwrng
```

To test this, we can use the od command, but maybe you should prefer using our new C interpreter with the following PicoC script:

```
#include <stdio.h>

FILE *f;
char buf[4];
int i;

f  = fopen("/dev/hwrng", "r");
fgets(buf, sizeof(buf), f);

for (i = 0; i < 4; i++)
    printf("%02x ", buf[i]);
printf("\n");
```

Just put the preceding code in a file named read_hwrng.picoc and execute it using the following command:

```
./picoc -s  read_hwrng.picoc
b2 9f 1c 00
```

 Note that the /dev/hwrng device is a random number generator, so the output changes each time we rerun the command.

Before ending this section, I'd like to remind you that, in case you wish to change the kernel configuration and then rebuild it, then the `build_kernel.sh` script should be changed, commenting out the line where the `FULL_REBUILD` variable is set. Here is the output from the `diff` command:

```
$ git diff build_kernel.sh
diff --git a/build_kernel.sh b/build_kernel.sh
index 84d68c2..7868d59 100755
--- a/build_kernel.sh
+++ b/build_kernel.sh
@@ -238,7 +238,7 @@ echo "debug: CC=${CC}"
 export LINUX_GIT


 #unset FULL_REBUILD
-FULL_REBUILD=1
+#FULL_REBUILD=1
 if [ "${FULL_REBUILD}" ] ; then
        /bin/sh -e "${DIR}/scripts/git.sh" || { exit 1 ; }
```

This will prevent the script from restarting the kernel compilation from the very beginning, thereby consequently saving of a lot of the developer's time.

# Device drivers

The Linux kernel holds by default a lot of device drivers, but it may happen that we need to install a recent one in the system not yet imported in the kernel tree for several reasons (for example, the driver is very new, or nobody asked for its insertion, or just because we write it by ourselves). In this case, we need to know some techniques on how a device driver can be compiled (advanced details about a device driver, and how it can be used to exchange data with a peripheral will be explained in detail in *Chapter 5, Device Drivers*). As for the user-space tool, the device driver compilation steps may vary and two major possibilities exist:

- The driver's source code is a patch to be applied to the kernel tree
- The driver's source code has a standard Makefile compatible with the Linux's one

The first case is quite simple. After the device driver's patch has been applied, the developer just needs to recompile the kernel, as mentioned earlier. In this case, the driver can be compiled as a kernel built-in or as kernel module.

A **kernel module** is a special binary file that can be inserted in the kernel at runtime when a specific functionality is requested. This prevents us from having a very large kernel image; in fact, we can select which functionalities are required since the boot and which ones can be loaded later on a demand basis.

For example, when a new device is inserted into the system, the kernel may ask you to load a kernel module that holds the corresponding device driver. However, a module may also be built as a monolithic part of the kernel (kernel built-in).

The first case is just a normal kernel recompilation, while the latter case is a bit more complex, but all the complexity is managed by the Makefile. The user has to properly configure it, and then execute the `make` command only.

When a device driver code is not merged into the kernel sources, the driver can be compiled as a kernel module only, that is, we cannot compile it statically into the kernel.

It's important to note that when a device driver is released as a separate package with a Makefile compatible with the Linux's one, we can compile it natively too. However, even in this case, we need to install a kernel source tree in the target machine anyways. Not only, but the sources must also be configured in the same manner as the running kernel or the resulting driver will not work at all.

This solution is not covered in this book, but you may look it up on the Internet or by reading the book, *Linux Device Drivers, Third Edition, O'Reilly Media* by Jonathan Corbet, Alessandro Rubini, and Greg Kroah-Hartman available at the bookshop and online at `http://lwn.net/Kernel/LDD3/`.

As an example of this special case, we'll take a look at a very simple dummy code that can simulate the activity of a device driver module in the kernel. Let's consider the following kernel code, and put this code in the `module.c` file in a working directory named `module`:

```
#include <linux/module.h>
#include <linux/init.h>

/* This is the function executed during the module loading */
static int dummy_module_init(void)
{
    printk("dummy_module loaded!\n");
    return 0;
}
```

```
/* This is the function executed during the module unloading */
static void dummy_module_exit(void)
{
        printk("dummy_module unloaded!\n");
        return;
}

module_init(dummy_module_init);
module_exit(dummy_module_exit);

MODULE_LICENSE("GPL");
```

Then, add a Makefile to the `module` directory that holds the following commands:

```
KERNEL_DIR ?= .      # to be set fro the command line

# This specifies the kernel module to be compiled
obj-m += module.o

# The default action
all: modules

# The main tasks
modules clean:
        make -C $(KERNEL_DIR) ARCH=arm CROSS_COMPILE=arm-linux-gnueabihf- \
                SUBDIRS=$(PWD) $@
```

After doing this, we will have the following files created in our working directory:

```
$ ls module/
Makefile   module.c
```

Well, our dummy driver can now be easily compiled by executing the following commands in the `module` directory:

```
$ cd module
$ make KERNEL_DIR=../linux-dev/KERNEL/ modules
make -C ../linux-dev/KERNEL/ ARCH=arm CROSS_COMPILE=arm-linux-gnueabihf- \
SUBDIRS=/home/giometti/Projects/packt/beagleboneblack/kernel/module modules
make[1]: Entering directory `/home/giometti/Projects/packt/beagleboneblack/
kernel/linux-dev/KERNEL'
  CC [M]  /home/giometti/Projects/packt/beagleboneblack/kernel/module/
module.o
  Building modules, stage 2.
  MODPOST 1 modules
```

```
   CC      /home/giometti/Projects/packt/beagleboneblack/kernel/module/
module.mod.o
   LD [M]   /home/giometti/Projects/packt/beagleboneblack/kernel/module/
module.ko
make[1]: Leaving directory `/home/giometti/Projects/packt/beagleboneblack/
kernel/linux-dev/KERNEL'
```

 Note that I specified the KERNEL_DIR path from the working
directory to the kernel's sources.

Now we have the following files in the working directory:

```
$ ls
Makefile           module.c      module.mod.c module.o
Module.symvers     module.ko     module.mod.o modules.order
```

Our new module is present in the module.ko file, so to test whether the compilation
has been correctly completed, let's copy it to our BeagleBone Black, and then insert it
into the kernel using the following command:

```
# insmod module.ko
```

On the serial console, we should see the following message:

```
dummy_module loaded!
```

Once we get this message, we can verify that the module has been loaded. Then,
the module can be unloaded using the rmmod module command.

If we are using a SSH connection or the kernel messages logging has been disabled,
we can see them using the tail or dmesg commands (see the *Managing the kernel
messages* section of *Chapter 2, Managing the System Console*, for more details).

# Summary

In this chapter, we saw and addressed several issues regarding the native
compilation and cross-compilation of both user-space and kernel-space.

This chapter was also a brief walkthrough on how to compile and cross-compile
files and the available software packages from a source.

Now, you should be more familiar with how to compile a C code from scratch; however, as already stated in this chapter, sometimes, it would be better to use a scripting language instead of a compiled C program. Well, in the next chapter, we'll see how we can use some powerful high-level scripting languages to quickly resolve several common tasks in our BeagleBone Black.

# 4
# Quick Programming with Scripts

In the previous chapter, we dealt with native compilation and cross-compilation, but sometimes, it is better to use a script to quickly solve a problem.

In this chapter, we will see how to install and use some common scripting languages in our new BeagleBone Black board, and then see how to solve a real problem by writing the solution in different languages (we'll present PHP, Python, and Bash) in order to show you the differences between them.

## The GPIO subsystem

In order to resolve a real problem, we first need to introduce you to one of the most used computer interfaces, the **General Purpose Input Output (GPIO)** interface. Using this interface, we can read or write some electrical statuses in the environment, which allows an interaction between the hardware and software. GPIO management has already been introduced in the *GPIOs management* section of *Chapter 2, Managing the System Console*. However, this time, the same GPIO subsystem is managed by the kernel, so the functions and commands that the developer can use to interact with the GPIOs (usually called **API**, that is, **application programming interface**) are quite different.

GPIO signals are very useful input/output lines that can be used for a large variety of tasks. In a common industrial application, these lines are normally used to manage relays and/or LEDs and to read the status of a switch and/or a photocell.

In this introduction, we'll present the API interface to manage these signals in a GNU/Linux system, and see how it can be used on our BeagleBone Black board to manage an LED over the network.

Even if the real problem we choose (managing an LED over the network) may appear quite simple, in reality, it's an optimal base to understand how the GPIO subsystem works and how a web application can get access to it. I'm quite sure that once you have finished reading this chapter, you will be more confident in using the presented tools in order to realize your first remote controlling application.

# The GPIOs on the BeagleBone Black

As already mentioned in the *A system overview* section of *Chapter 1, Installing the Developing System*, the BeagleBone Black has two expansion connectors, where several signals are exposed and where we can find several GPIO pins, as shown in the following table:

| GPIO pins on connector P8 | | GPIO pins on connector P9 | |
|---|---|---|---|
| Pin | GPIO # | Pin | GPIO # |
| 7 | 66 | 12 | 60 |
| 8 | 67 | 15 | 48 |
| 9 | 69 | 23 | 49 |
| 10 | 68 | 25 | 117 |
| 11 | 45 | 27 | 115 |
| 12 | 44 | 30 | 112 |
| 14 | 26 | 41 | 20 |
| 15 | 47 | | |
| 16 | 46 | | |
| 17 | 27 | | |
| 18 | 65 | | |
| 6 | 61 | | |
| 1 and 2 | GND | 1 and 2 | GND |

A complete BeagleBone Black's connectors description is available at
http://elinux.org/Beagleboard:Cape_Expansion_Headers.

For our simple example, we can use one of these lines connected with an LED, as
shown in the following image:

I just connected the LED with the GPIO line number 66 (named gpio66), that is,
with pin **7** of connector **P8** (**P8.7**).

Note that the LEDs anode must be connected to pin **7** of connector **P8**
(**P8.7**) and the cathode with the GND or ground (pin **1** or **2** of the same
connector). Let me also recall that the flat spot on the LED is the cathode
while the rounded one is the anode.

A careful reader with a minimum electronic basics will notice that I did
not put any resistance in series with the LED to limit the output current
from the GPIO pin. Even if it should be always done to avoid damages, I
decided to not put it to keep the connection very simple.

As stated before, I used an LED, but we can use whatever we wish to be managed by our BeagleBone Black. We only need to take care of what we connect to the board in order to avoid damages.

# The sysfs API

Now it's time to explain the **application programming interface (API)** we can use to manage the gpio66 chosen earlier.

In perfect Unix style, where everything is a file, all GPIOs are exposed as files in the system, more precisely, they are directories in the sysfs filesystem, which is a virtual filesystem mounted under the /sys directory by default at boot.

> A **virtual filesystem** is a filesystem that contains virtual files (files stored nowhere that are filled with information created on the fly when they are accessed) used to export information about various kernel subsystems, hardware devices, and associated device drivers to user space. Not only that, in addition to providing this information, these exported virtual files are also used for system configuration and device management.
>
> You may get more information by surfing the Internet or just reading the linux/Documentation/filesystems/sysfs.txt file in Linux's source tree.

Each GPIO has its related files exposed under the /sys/class/gpio directory. On the BeagleBone Black, we have the following:

```
root@BeagleBone:~# ls /sys/class/gpio
export  gpiochip0  gpiochip32  gpiochip64  gpiochip96  unexport
```

The files named gpiochipXX are related to the GPIO controllers that are defined in the system, while the export and unexport files can be used to export and unexport a GPIO line to the user space. For example, let's see how to export gpio66 by simply writing the string 66 in the export file as follows:

```
root@BeagleBone:~# echo 66 > /sys/class/gpio/export
```

This command is will execute an open() system call, and then a write() system call in the file. In C, we can use something like this:

```
f = fopen("/sys/class/gpio/export", "w");
fprintf(f, "66\n");
fclose(f);
```

Note that the fopen() and fwrite() functions call the open() and write() system calls respectively. While the fclose() function, which, in turn, calls the close() function, is used to force the file writing to effectively set the GPIO line to the desired status. This is because fwrite() and fread() are buffered, that is, they cache the data before writing, and a good practice would be not to use them for accessing GPIOs. Technically, stuff such as GPIOs should always be written using open() and read() so that they do the required operation in a predictable way.

After running the preceding command, we get a new directory named gpio66 that stores the following files:

```
root@BeagleBone:~# ls /sys/class/gpio/gpio66/
active_low  direction  edge  power  subsystem  uevent  value
```

The currently configured GPIO direction is stored in the direction file (that is, if the GPIO is an input or an output), and the mode must be set properly, otherwise if someone accidentally applies an input to a pin set in the output mode, it can damage the board beyond repair. If we read the direction file content, we get the following:

```
root@BeagleBone:~# cat /sys/class/gpio/gpio66/direction
in
```

Alternatively, we can write the preceding command in C language as follows:

```
f = fopen("/sys/class/gpio/gpio66/direction", "r");
fscanf(f, "%c", &d);
fclose(f);
```

Here, the GPIO variable is stored in the char variable d. The character i or o is stored depending on whether it is an input or output direction.

Note that the fscan() function calls the read() system call, while fopen() and fclose() work as before.

The preceding output shows that `gpio66` is an input pin; however, we need it to be an output pin because we need to turn our LED on and off, so let's change the pin configuration by writing the `out` string in the `direction` file as follows:

```
root@BeagleBone:~# echo out > /sys/class/gpio/gpio66/direction
```

Now we can read the current output pin status by reading the `value` file as follows:

```
root@BeagleBone:~# cat /sys/class/gpio/gpio66/value
0
```

The preceding output shows that the output pin is at a lower level, and in turn, the LED is off; to turn it on, we must write `1` in the preceding file:

```
root@BeagleBone:~# echo 1 > /sys/class/gpio/gpio66/value
```

Now our LED should be on.

# Managing an LED in PHP

Now it's time to see how to manage our LED using the PHP language.

There are two different possibilities to do this: the first one is to use the **LAMP (Linux-Apache-MySQL-PHP)** system we set up in *The LAMP suite* section of *Chapter 1, Installing the Developing System*, while the second one is to use the PHP built-in web server.

## The LAMP solution

This is the easiest and most classic way to implement a common web application. We just need a PHP script where we can implement our LED management. So let's start with writing some code!

In the first step, we must create a file named `turn.php` in the `/var/www/` directory of the BeagleBone Black with the following content:

```php
<?php
        # 1st part - Global defines & functions
        define("value_f", "/sys/class/gpio/gpio66/value");

        # 2nd part - Get the current led status
        $led_status = intval(file_get_contents(value_f));

        # 3rd part - Render the led status by HTML code
    ?>
```

```html
<html>
  <head>
    <title>Turning a led on/off using PHP</title>
  </head>

  <body>
    <h1>Turning a led on/off using PHP</h1>

    Current led status is: <? echo $led_status ? "on" : "off" ?>
  </body>
</html>
```

> Note that this code does not export the gpio66 directory, so it must be exported, as shown in the previous section, before running the script.
>
> The code is stored in the chapter_04/webled/php/turn_1st.php file in the book's example code repository.

The function is quite simple; the first part of the code reads the LED status and stores it in the led_status variable, while the second part is an HTML code with mixed PHP code that is needed to simply report the LED status by echoing the led_status variable. However, if we wish to toggle the LED status, we have to add the logic to permit the user to do it by modifying the code as follows:

```diff
--- turn_1st.php        2015-04-02 17:31:42.652320166 +0200
+++ turn_2nd.php        2015-04-02 17:31:59.796320996 +0200
@@ -2,10 +2,24 @@
    # 1st part - Global defines & functions
    define("value_f", "/sys/class/gpio/gpio66/value");

-   # 2nd part - Get the current led status
+   function pr_str($val)
+   {
+       echo $val ? "on" : "off";
+   }
+
+   # 2nd part - Set the new led status as requested
+   if (isset($_GET["led"])) {
+       $led_new_status = $_GET["led"];
+       file_put_contents(value_f, $led_new_status);
+   }
+
+   # 3rd part - Get the current led status
```

```
     $led_status = intval(file_get_contents(value_f));

-    # 3rd part - Render the led status by HTML code
+    # 4th part - Logic to change the led status on the next call
+    $led_new_status = 1 - $led_status;
+
+    # 5th part - Render the led status by HTML code
 ?>
 <html>
   <head>
@@ -14,7 +28,16 @@

   <body>
     <h1>Turning a led on/off using PHP</h1>
+    Current led status is: <? pr_str($led_status) ?>
+    <p>
+
+    Press the button to turn the led <? pr_str($led_new_status) ?>
+    <p>
+
+    <form method="get" action="/turn.php">
+      <button type="submit" value="<? echo $led_new_status ?>"
+          name="led">Turn <? pr_str($led_new_status) ?></button>
+    </form>

-    Current led status is: <? echo $led_status ? "on" : "off" ?>
   </body>
 </html>
```

 The complete code is stored in the `chapter_04/webled/php/turn_2nd.php` file in the book's example code repository.

This time, the code is a bit more complex but is still very simple. In the first part, we have the same definition as before, a new function is used to convert a number to the on or off string. In the second part, we have the code written to retrieve the user request, that is, if we have to turn the LED on or off, and then execute it.

Note that the user request is done with an HTTP GET request in the following form:

`http://192.168.7.2/turn.php?led=1`

Note that we used the USB Ethernet emulation to get access to the BeagleBone Black's LAMP system, as presented in *The SSH tool* section of *Chapter 1, Installing the Developing System*.

The `led=1` string asks the function to turn the LED on, so the code gets this value, and using the PHP `file_put_contents()` function, we can set the LED on by writing 1 in the `/sys/class/gpio/gpio66/value` file.

The third part is similar to before, while the fourth one just toggles the LED status from the value 0 to 1 or vice versa.

The fifth part is the HTML page that the server will return to the user with the current LED status and the needed button to toggle it. The following screenshot shows the resulting output in the browser:

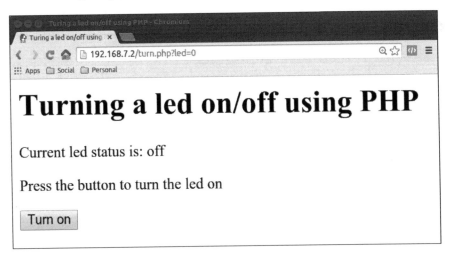

It may happen that the code cannot change the LED status; in this case, we should check the `/var/log/apache2/error.log` file, where the Apache web server logs the possible errors:

If we see an error message, as shown in the following code, the problem is due to a file permission issue:

```
[Thu Apr 24 02:15:38 2014] [error] [client 192.168.7.1] PHP Warning:
file_put_contents(/sys/class/gpio/gpio66/value): failed to open
stream: Permission denied in /var/www/turn.php on line 18, referer:
http://192.168.7.2/turn.php?led=1
```

So, let's check the file permission for the `/sys/class/gpio/gpio66/value` file:

```
root@BeagleBone:/var/www# ls -l /sys/class/gpio/gpio66/value
-rw-r--r-- 1 root root 4096 Apr 24 02:15 /sys/class/gpio/gpio66/value
```

As supposed, only the root user has the right privileges to write into the file, so a possible workaround could be as follows:

```
root@BeagleBone:/var/www# chown :www-data /sys/class/gpio/gpio66/value
root@BeagleBone:/var/www# chmod g+rw /sys/class/gpio/gpio66/value
root@BeagleBone:/var/www# ls -l /sys/class/gpio/gpio66/value
-rw-rw-r-- 1 root www-data 4096 Apr 24 02:20 /sys/class/gpio/gpio66/value
```

This is because the Apache web server runs with the same privileges as the `www-data` user and `www-data` group, but after the preceding changes, our script should work as expected.

# The built-in server solution

The PHP built-in web server can be executed with the following command line:

```
root@BeagleBone:~# php -S 192.168.7.2:8080 -t /var/www/
PHP 5.4.4-14+deb7u14 Development Server started at Fri Apr 25 16:19:05 2014
Listening on 192.168.7.2:8080
Document root is /var/www
Press Ctrl-C to quit.
```

You should notice that I used the listening address `192.168.7.2:8080`, so this time, the web address to be used is `http://192.168.7.2:8080/turn.php`, otherwise we will get connected to the Apache server again!

If we wish to avoid specifying the port `8080`, we should stop the Apache web server as follows:

```
root@BeagleBone:~# /etc/init.d/apache2 stop
[ ok ] Stopping apache2 (via systemctl): apache2.service.
```

Then, rerun the PHP built-in web server with the following command:

```
php -S 192.168.7.2:80 -t /var/www/
```

Now we can execute our script as before. Note that the server will log each browser request on the terminal where it's running:

```
[Fri Apr 25 16:35:58 2014] 192.168.7.1:43412 [200]: /turn.php
[Fri Apr 25 16:36:01 2014] 192.168.7.1:43413 [200]: /turn.php?led=1
[Fri Apr 25 16:36:02 2014] 192.168.7.1:43414 [200]: /turn.php?led=0
```

 As reported in the PHP built-in web server's manual at http://php.net/manual/en/features.commandline.webserver.php, this tool should be used for testing purposes or for application demonstrations that are run in controlled environments only.

# Managing an LED in Python

Now let's try to manage our LED using a Python script. There are several possibilities to get a running web server with Python, but the easiest one is definitely the BaseHTTPServer library.

You can refer to a simple usage of the library in the chapter_04/webled/python/httpd_show_info.py demo script in the book's example code repository, where we will show you how the server handler processes the incoming requests by showing all the fields available at the disposal of the programmer.

The first part displays the definition of the server listening address, while the second part defines the GET requests handler, that is, the function to be called each time the browser performs an HTTP GET request.

The third and fourth parts are the most important ones since they implement the web data parsing. Here, we can see how the web requests are managed, and how we can use them to do our job. The fourth part simply takes the answering message built by the third part and then sends it back to the browser. Let's take a look at the following snippet of the relevant function:

```
def do_GET(self):
    parsed_path = urlparse.urlparse(self.path)

    # 3rd part - Build the answering message
    message_parts = [
        'CLIENT VALUES',
        'client_address -> %s (%s)' % (self.client_address,
```

```
                                          self.address_string()),
        'command -> %s' % self.command,
        'path -> %s' % self.path,
        'real path -> t%s' % parsed_path.path,
        'query -> %s' % parsed_path.query,
        'request_version -> %s' % self.request_version,
        '',
        'SERVER VALUES',
        'server_version -> %s' % self.server_version,
        'sys_version -> %s' % self.sys_version,
        'protocol_version -> %s' % self.protocol_version,
        '',
        'HEADERS RECEIVED',
    ]

    for name, value in sorted(self.headers.items()):
        message_parts.append('%s -> %s' % (name,
                value.rstrip()))
    message_parts.append('')
    message = '\r\n'.join(message_parts)

    # 4th part - Send the answer
    self.send_response(200)
    self.end_headers()
    self.wfile.write(message)

    return
```

The last part is executed at the beginning, and it sets up the server by creating a new server object by calling the HTTPServer() function and then runs it by calling the serve_forever() method.

To test the code, we can use the following command:

```
root@BeagleBone:~# python httpd_show_info.py
Starting server at 192.168.7.2:8080, use <Ctrl-C> to stop
```

If everything works well, we'll see the server running by pointing the browser to the http://192.168.7.2:8080/?led=1 address.

The output in the browser should look something like this:

As we can see, there are tons of available data; however, to manage our LED, we can just use the `query` variable, that is, where the server stores the HTTP GET request data. You can find a possible implementation of our LED management script in Python in the `chapter_04/webled/python/httpd.py` file in the book's example code repository.

This time, the code is really more complex than before. Note that in the first part of this new code, I've defined two functions: `put_data()` and `get_data()`. These are used to put/get the `gpio66` status. Here, the snippet with these two functions is as follows:

```
def put_data(file, data):
        f = open(file, "w")
        f.write(data)
```

```
                    f.close()

    def get_data(file):
            f = open(file, "r")
            data = f.read()
            f.close()
            return data
```

The second part is not changed while the third one has now been changed in order to retrieve the HTTP GET query and sets up the new `gpio66` status accordingly.

The fourth and fifth parts are very similar to their respective ones in PHP, and the same goes for the sixth one too, even if its layout is a bit different (it defines the HTML code to be returned to the browser).

The seventh part is the same as before while the eighth part implements the server definition and initialization.

If we execute this new script as we did earlier, we should get the same output we got with the PHP version of this script.

# Managing an LED in Bash

Both Python and PHP languages are very powerful, and they can be used to solve a lot of complex problems; however, it may happen that the embedded system lacks both. In this case, we can use the C language or, if we like scripting, we can try to use Bash.

In fact, even if the Bash scripting language is commonly used to solve the system administrator's tasks, it can be also used to resolve several issues with some tricks. So, let's see how we can use it in our web LED management problem.

By default, Bash has no networking features; however, as a workaround, we can use the **inetd** daemon. This tool is a network daemon program that specializes in adding networking features to programs that normally don't have these features. Its configuration file `/etc/inetd.conf` tells Bash which program needs to be run when an incoming network connection is received, but before doing it, it redirects the program's **stdin**, **stdout**, and **stderr** streams to the socket used to manage the connection. By doing this, every program that simply writes and reads data to and from the standard Unix streams can talk remotely over a network connection.

It's more difficult to explain this than to show you an example, so let give me you a simple example.

First of all, we need to install the daemon on our BeagleBone Black along with the networking tool `telnet` using the following command:

**root@BeagleBone:~# aptitude install openbsd-inetd telnet**

Now consider the following Bash script:

```
#!/bin/bash

while /bin/true; do
        read line

        line=$(echo $line | tr -d '\n\r')
        [ "$line" == "quit" ] && break;

        echo -e "$line\r"
done

exit 0
```

 The code is stored in the `chapter_04/webled/bash/` `echo_1st.sh` file in the book's example code repository.

If we try to run it, we get the following output:

**root@BeagleBone:~# ./echo_1st.sh**

Now if we try to enter the `Testing request` string, the script will echo it on its **stdout** (that is, on the terminal window). Then, to exit the program, we must enter the `quit` string. Here is a simple usage:

**root@BeagleBone:~# ./echo_1st.sh**

**Testing request**

**Testing request**

**quit**

**root@BeagleBone:~#**

Now if we add the following line in the `inetd` configuration file (that is, the `/etc/` `inetd.conf` file), we can test the `inetd` functionality:

```
8080                    stream  tcp  nowait  root  /root/echo_1st.sh
```

By adding this line, the file contents should look like this (only the last four lines are shown in the following snippet):

```
#:HAM-RADIO: amateur-radio services

#:OTHER: Other services
8080                            stream  tcp  nowait  root  /root/echo_1st.sh
```

Now we must restart the daemon to activate the new settings:

```
root@BeagleBone:~# /etc/init.d/openbsd-inetd restart
[ ok ] Restarting openbsd-inetd (via systemctl): openbsd-inetd.service.
```

In the first step, we can verify that the daemon is really listening on port 8080 as expected:

```
root@BeagleBone:~# netstat -lpn | grep 8080
tcp        0      0 0.0.0.0:8080              0.0.0.0:*
LISTEN       2124/inetd
```

Now to test the real magic of this daemon, we have to use the telnet command as follows:

```
root@BeagleBone:~# telnet localhost 8080
Trying 127.0.0.1...
Connected to localhost.
Escape character is '^]'.
```

At this point, let's try to re-enter the Testing request string as before. Great! Our program is answering using a network connection.

Now we can play with it, insert whatever we want, and then use the quit string to close the connection.

> Note that we can use the telnet command from the host PC too. In this manner, we may convince ourselves that the Bash script is really working over the network.

The trick, as stated earlier, correctly set up the inetd configuration file; in fact, by adding the previous configuration line, we asked the inetd file to listen on TCP port 8080 for a new incoming connection, and after answering and redirecting the standard Unix streams to the socket, to execute our script.

Now, using the same trick, and of course, using a modified script, we can rewrite a new solution for our web LED management problem.

First of all, we should know exactly what the browser asks a web server. To do this, we can use a modified version of our echo program, as shown in the following snippet:

```bash
#!/bin/bash

# The server's root directory
base=/var/www

# Read the browser request
read request

# Now read the message header
while /bin/true; do
        read header
        echo "$header"
        [ "$header" == $'\r' ] && break;
done

# And then produce an answer with a message dump
echo -e "HTTP/1.1 200 OK\r"
echo -e "Content-type: text/html\r"
echo -e "\r"

echo -e "request=$request\r"

exit 0
```

 The code is stored in the `chapter_04/webled/bash/echo_2nd.sh` file in the book's example code repository.

This new script is quite simple; it first reads the browser's request, then it starts reading the message header, and when finished, it produces an answer with a message dump, so we can analyze it and understand what they say to each other.

Now if we modify the `inetd` configuration file in order to execute the `echo_2nd.sh` program instead of the `echo_1st.sh` program, by pointing our web browser to the address `http://192.168.7.2:8080/index.html`, we will see a message like the following code snippet:

```
Host: 192.168.7.2:8080
Connection: keep-alive
Accept: text/html,application/xhtml+xml,application/xml;q=0.9,image/
webp,*/*;q=0.8
```

```
User-Agent: Mozilla/5.0 (X11; Linux x86_64) AppleWebKit/537.36
(KHTML, like Gecko) Ubuntu Chromium/39.0.2171.65 Chrome/39.0.2171.65
Safari/537.36
```

```
Accept-Encoding: gzip, deflate, sdch
```

```
Accept-Language: en-US,en;q=0.8,it;q=0.6
```

```
HTTP/1.1 200 OK
```

```
Content-type: text/html
```

```
request=GET /index.html HTTP/1.1
```

The first seven lines are the message headers, then there are two lines with the server's answer, and in the end, we have the dump of the initial request. As we can see, the browser did an HTTP GET Version 1.1 request, asking for the /index.html file. So, our Bash web server should simply read the browser's request, then skip the header, and in the end, return the contents of the file specified in the request.

A possible implementation is reported in the chapter_04/webled/bash/httpd_nocgi.sh file. So, we have only to configure the inetd daemon accordingly using the following configuration line:

```
8080                    stream   tcp    nowait   root    /root/httpd_nocgi.sh
```

Now, after restarting the daemon, we can try our new web server written in the Bash language.

To test the server, we need an index.html file in the web server's root directory /var/www so that we can add a file that has the following HTML code:

```
<html>
  <head>
    <title>HTML index file</title>
  </head>

  <body>
    <h1>Hello World!!!</h1>
  </body>
</html>
```

Now everything is in place; if we point our web browser to the BeagleBone Black IP address as done before, we will get the index.html file contents: the famous string Hello World!!!. Nice, isn't it?

However, we have not finished as yet; in fact, in order to implement our web LED management using Bash, we need to have the ability to execute a script from the web server. Well, this is quite easy if we modify our code as follows:

```
root@BeagleBone:~# diff -u httpd_nocgi.sh httpd_cgi.sh
--- httpd_nocgi.sh  2014-04-23 22:34:37.255860337 +0000
+++ httpd.sh  2014-04-23 22:35:50.876954096 +0000
@@ -16,6 +16,10 @@
 tmp="${request#GET }"
 tmp="${tmp% HTTP/*}"

+# Extract the code after the '?' char to capture a variable setting
+var="${tmp#*\?}"
+[ "$var" == "$tmp" ] && var=""
+
 # Get the URL and replace it with "/index.html" in case it is set to "/"
 url="${tmp%\?*}"
 [ "$url" == "/" ] && url="/index.html"
@@ -29,7 +33,14 @@
     echo -e "HTTP/1.1 200 OK\r"
     echo -e "Contant-type: text/html\r"
     echo -e "\r"
-    cat "$filename"
+
+    # If file's extension is "cgi" and it's executable the execute it,
+    # otherwise just return its contents
+    if [ "$extension" == "cgi" -a -x "$filename" ]; then
+        $filename $var
+    else
+        cat "$filename"
+    fi
     echo -e "\r"
   else
     # If the file does not exist return an error
```

The complete code is stored in the `chapter_04/webled/bash/httpd_cgi.sh` file in the book's example code repository.

That is, instead of using the `cat` command to simply return the file content, we will first verify that the file has the `cgi` extension, and if it's executable; in this case, we will simply execute it.

Note that before doing this, we need to extract the code after the `?` character in order to get the variable settings when we use a URL in the form `http://192.168.7.2:8080/?led=1`. This task is done by the `var="${tmp#*\?}"` code.

Ok, now the final version of the web server is ready, but to complete the server-side actions, we need to add a CGI functionality.

A possible CGI implementation is stored in the `chapter_04/webled/bash/turn.cgi` file in the book's example code repository, and the following snippet of the relevant functions shows where the LED status is managed:

```
# 2nd part - Set the new led status as requested
if [ -n "$1" ] ; then
    eval $1      ;# this evaluate the query 'led=0'
    led_new_status = $led
    echo $led_new_status > $value_f
fi

led_status=$(cat $value_f)

led_new_status=$((1 - $led_status))
```

Now everything is really in place! If we point the browser, as we did for the PHP and the Python version of our LED management code, we should get a similar function as before.

Note that the Bash web server presented here is not a strictly compliant web server nor a safe one! Even if it can work in most cases, it's just a simple demonstration program, and it shouldn't be used in a production environment.

In these Bash examples, we used some special syntaxes, which may be obscure to you (especially for beginners). Maybe a look at a Bash tutorial may help you. A good starting point is at `http://tldp.org/HOWTO/Bash-Prog-Intro-HOWTO.html`.

# Summary

In this chapter, we discovered that several scripting languages can be used on our BeagleBone Black in order to simplify our job as developers. We discovered the GPIO subsystem, and we learned how to manage the digital input/output signals. We also learned that the `inetd` daemon can be used to add networking capabilities to any applications by redirecting its standard streams to a networking socket.

In the next chapter, we'll present other daemons, and we'll also learn how to write our own daemon in order to do repetitive tasks.

# 5
# Device Drivers

In the previous chapter, we saw how to manage a LED from a remote PC, and then we used a dedicated web server to manage the LED remotely. In order to do this, we introduced the BeagleBone Black's GPIO subsystem; however, tons of different kinds of computer peripherals exist, so now it's time to recall what we saw in the homonyms section in the *Device drivers* section of *Chapter 3, Compiling versus Cross-compiling*, and try to focus our attention a bit more in-depth on what a device driver is and how it can be used.

After a brief introduction of the device driver concept, we'll see a possible implementation of a very simple driver (by writing a proper kernel module) in order to show you the Linux kernel's internals, and then, starting from the next chapter, we'll present different kinds of computer peripherals, and for each of them, we'll try to explain how the corresponding device driver works, starting from the compilation stage, through the configuration, until the usage stage.

## What is a device driver?

A **device driver** is a special code that interfaces a physical device into the system and exports it to the user-space processes using a well-defined API. In an Unix-like OS, where everything is a file (see the following section), the physical device is represented as a file, and then the device driver implements all the system calls a process can do on a file.

The difference between a normal function and a system call is just the fact that the latter is mainly executed in the kernel while a function executes in the user space only.

For example, `printf()` is a function while `write()` is a system call. The latter (except for a prologue and an epilogue) executes in the kernel space while the former executes in the user space (even if it calls the `write()` function to actually write its data to the output stream).

The system calls are used to communicate with the peripherals and other processes and to get access to the kernel internals data. This is why a system call triggers a switch from the user space to kernel space, where the important code is executed, and after the execution, the code is switched back to the user space to execute the normal code. For this reason, the code that is executed in the kernel space is considered a code that executes in a privileged mode.

For example, let's consider the GPIO subsystem we used in the previous chapter; for each GPIO line, we have a directory called `/sys/class/gpio/gpioXX/`, where we can find the `value` and `direction` files. Each `read()` system call on the value file (for example, by running the `cat /sys/class/gpio/gpio66/value` command) is translated by the kernel in the `gpio_read()` kernel method that actually does the reading of the `gpio66` status:

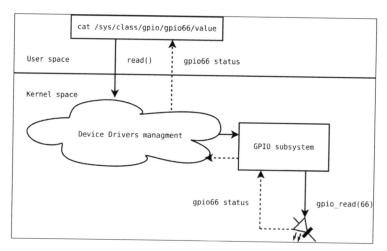

The same happens, for instance, when we do a `read()` system call on another file under the `/dev` directory, the kernel translates the `read()` system call to the corresponding device driver's method that actually executes the reading.

Note that the system call is always the same (the `read()` function), but in the kernel, the right method is called each time. You can imagine that this mechanism works like an object programming language: the `read()` method is a method that operates in a different manner according to the object (device) passed to it. For more information on how this complex mechanism exactly works, and for everything about the device drivers in Linux, you can take a look at the book, *Linux Device Drivers, Third Edition*, available at the bookshop and online at `http://lwn.net/Kernel/LDD3/`.

# Char, block, and net devices

In the Linux kernel, the following three major device types exist:

- **char device**: This kind of device groups all the peripherals that can be accessed as a stream of bytes such as a file (that is, serial ports, audio devices, and so on). A char driver is in charge of implementing this behavior usually by implementing at least the `open()`, `close()`, `read()`, and `write()` system calls.

- **block device**: This kind of device groups all the peripherals that can host a filesystem, so it is accessed as a block of bytes (usually 512, or a larger power of two).

- **net device**: This kind of device groups all the peripherals that can manage a network transaction. It is different from the char and block devices, as this special device has no related filesystem nodes, such as `/dev/ttyACM0` or `/dev/sdb1`.

A driver interfacing a char device is usually called a **char driver**, while a driver for a block device is called a **block driver**, and of course, the **net driver** is the driver for a net device.

Despite these three major groups, in the recent kernel releases, we can find several subgroups (or classes) of device drivers, which are still based in one of the preceding major groups but are specialized to manage a particular device type.

For instance, the real-time clock devices are represented by a dedicated device driver class defined under the `/drivers/rtc` directory in the Linux source tree. In the same manner, the **pulse per second** (**PPS**) devices have a dedicated device driver class defined under the `/drivers/pps` directory, and the same for the input devices (mouse, keyboard, and so on) are defined under the `/drivers/input` directory, and so on.

All these specific device drivers are implemented using the char drivers.

 In the next sections, we cannot explain in-depth how all of these device drivers classes are implemented since it's out of the scope of this book; however, we'll try to give you all the information you need to configure and use them according to the peripherals we are going to show.

Another way to interact with a device is to use the `sysfs` filesystem. Strictly speaking, this not a device driver, but an in-memory representation of the device's internals whose permits anyway to get accessed it in a simple and clean way using the file abstraction (that is, everything is a file).

Remember that we already saw this special driver implementation in *The sysfs API* section of *Chapter 4, Quick Programming with Scripts*, when we managed a LED. In this chapter, we will go further; we are going to see how to write our own device driver using this interface in order to show you how powerful this system can be.

Everything is a file. This concept may appear quite exotic, but, in reality, it's very powerful. Let's consider what we did in the previous chapter with our LED. We managed the LED status from the PHP, Python, and BASH script in the same manner; we simply read and wrote data from/to a file.

To get the LED status, we didn't use a special code or dedicated functions at all, we simply used the same function that we used to read from a file. In PHP, we did the following:

```php
$led_status = intval(file_get_contents(value_f));
```

If we take a look at the `file_get_contents()` user manual, we can read the following:

*file_get_contents – Reads entire file into a string*

In Python, we did the following:

```python
def get_data(file):
        f = open(file, "r")
        data = f.read()
        f.close()
        return data
```

We used the `open()` and `read()` functions used to manage a file. In fact, in their user manual, we get the following output:

> *Open a file, returning an object of the file type described in section File Objects.*

> *To read a file's contents, call f.read(size), which reads some quantity of data and returns it as a string.*

In BASH, we did the following:

```
led_status=$(cat $value_f)
```

In the `cat` user manual, we read it:

> cat *— concatenates the files and prints them on the standard output. So, in all cases, the user manual talks about files.*

# The modutils

As we already saw in the *Device drivers* section of *Chapter 3, Compiling versus Cross-compiling*, a loadable kernel module can act as a device driver, and the system can load it at runtime when its functionalities are required. The basic command to load a module into the kernel is `insmod`; however, there exists another command to load a module (and its dependencies) and its name is `modprobe` (see the following section for more information).

Actually, there exists a group of commands to manage the kernel modules; these commands are called the **modutils**. On the Debian system, running on our BeagleBone Black, the modutils are stored in the package named `kmod`:

```
root@BeagleBone:~# apt-cache show kmod
Package: kmod
Version: 9-3
Installed-Size: 172
Maintainer: Marco d'Itri <md@linux.it>
Architecture: armhf
Replaces: module-init-tools (<< 4)
Depends: libc6 (>= 2.13-28), libgcc1 (>= 1:4.4.0), libkmod2 (>= 6~), lsb-base (>= 3.0-6)
Breaks: module-init-tools (<< 4)
Description-en: tools for managing Linux kernel modules
```

```
This package contains a set of programs for loading, inserting, and
removing kernel modules for Linux.
It replaces module-init-tools....
```

The available commands into the preceding package can be listed as:

```
root@BeagleBone:~# dpkg -L kmod | grep sbin\/
/sbin/insmod
/sbin/depmod
/sbin/modprobe
/sbin/rmmod
/sbin/lsmod
/sbin/modinfo
```

Let's take a look at these commands in detail:

- There is nothing to say about the `insmod` command than we already know; that it loads a module into the kernel.

- The `lsmod` command shows the user all the currently modules loaded into the kernel. By running it on my BeagleBone Black I get:

```
root@BeagleBone:~# lsmod
Module                   Size  Used by
usb_f_acm                5391  1
u_serial                10388  1 usb_f_acm
usb_f_ecm                6791  1
g_multi                  5412  0
usb_f_mass_storage      36667  2 g_multi
usb_f_rndis              7486  2 g_multi
u_rndis                  8696  1 usb_f_rndis
u_ether                 12790  3 usb_f_ecm,usb_f_rndis,g_multi
libcomposite            34723  5 usb_f_acm,usb_f_ecm,usb_f_rndis,g_
multi,usb_f_mass_storage
ti_am335x_adc            4679  0
kfifo_buf                2437  1 ti_am335x_adc
industrialio            46516  2 ti_am335x_adc,kfifo_buf
rtc_omap                 5276  0
uio_pdrv_genirq          3289  0
uio                      8910  1 uio_pdrv_genirq
```

The first column displays all the modules currently loaded in the system, the second column displays the module size in bytes, while the third column displays the use count by other modules, which are listed in the fourth column.

- The modprobe command is more complex than insmod because it can handle the dependencies of the module; that is, it can load all the modules needed by the user requested one to run.

  For example, let's see again the preceding output of the lsmod command. The column labeled Used by displays the name of the modules that are currently using the one in the first column. So, for instance, the g_multi module needs libcomposite to work.

  Well, modprobe is smart enough to know such a dependency, so when we execute the following command, the system will load libcomposite first and then g_multi:

  ```
  # modprobe g_multi
  ```

- The depmod command can be used to build a dependencies table suitable for the modprobe command.

I'm sorry but explaining how this mechanism works in detail is out of the scope of this book. You can take a look at the man pages of depmod using the man depmod command.

- The rmmod command can be used to unload a module from the system, releasing the RAM and other resources taken during its usage.

Note that this can be done only if the module is not actually used by any other module in the system; this fact is true only when the number in the *Used by* column in the preceding output of the lsmod command is equal to 0.

# Writing our own device driver

In the previous chapter, we made use of the GPIO subsystem of the kernel to manage a LED, now we'll go further to manage the GPIOs from the kernel using a dedicated driver. Actually, what we are going to write is not properly a driver for a real device, but we can use it in order to show you how a complex kernel functionality can be abstracted as a file.

Let's suppose we need to count some pulses that arrive on our BeagleBone Black in a certain amount of time; in this case, we can use one GPIO for each pulse source. We can also consider that the maximum possible pulse frequency is really low (max 50 Hz).

 Note that this situation is quite common, and it can be found in some counter devices. In fact, these devices simply count quantities (water or oil liters, energy power, and so on), and return the counting as frequency modulated pulses.

In this situation, we can use a really simple kernel code to implement a new devices class under the `sysfs` filesystem that we can use to abstract these measurements to the user space. Using our new driver, the user will see a new class named `pulse` and a new directory per device, where you can read the actual counting:

Here is a simple example of the final result:

```
root@BeagleBone:~# tree -l -L 2 /sys/class/pulse/
/sys/class/pulse/
|-- oil -> ../../devices/virtual/pulse/oil
|   |-- counter
|   |-- counter_and_reset
|   |-- gpio
|   |-- power
|   |-- set_to
|   |-- subsystem -> ../../../../class/pulse  [recursive, not followed]
|   `-- uevent
`-- water -> ../../devices/virtual/pulse/water
    |-- counter
    |-- counter_and_reset
    |-- gpio
    |-- power
    |-- set_to
    |-- subsystem -> ../../../../class/pulse  [recursive, not followed]
    `-- uevent

6 directories, 10 files
```

> Note that the tool tree can be installed by using the
> following command:
>
> ```
> root@BeagleBone:~# aptitude install tree
> ```

In the preceding example, we have two pulse devices named `oil` and `water`, represented by the directories with the same name, and for each device, four attributes files named: `counter`, `counter_and_reset`, `gpio`, and `set_to` (the other files named `power` and `subsystem` are not of interest to us).

You can now use the `counter` file to read the counting data; while using the `counter_and_reset` file, you can do the same as with the `counter` file, but after reading the data, the counter is automatically reset to the `0` value. Using the `set_to` file, you can initialize the counter to a specific value different from 0, while the `gpio` file is simply an information file that displays the BeagleBone Black's GPIO pin number used to get the pulse signal.

Now, before we continue to describe the driver, let me explain the code.

We have four files and the first one is the `Makefile`, as shown in the following code:

```
KERNEL_DIR := .            # to be set from the command line
PWD := $(shell pwd)
CROSS_COMPILE = arm-linux-gnueabihf-

obj-m = pulse.o
obj-m += pulse-bbb.o

all: modules

modules clean:
    $(MAKE) -C $(KERNEL_DIR) ARCH=arm CROSS_COMPILE=$(CROSS_COMPILE) \
        SUBDIRS=$(PWD) $@
```

> The code is stored in the `chapter_05/pulse/Makefile` file
> in the book's example code repository.

As we can see, it's quite similar to the one presented in the *Device drivers* section of *Chapter 3, Compiling versus Cross-compiling*, the only difference is the `obj-m` variable; in fact, this time, it declares two object files: `pulse.o` and `pulse-bbb.o`.

The `pulse-bbb.o` file can obviously be obtained by compiling the `pulse-bbb.c` file that holds the definition of the two pulse devices named `oil` and `water`. In fact, as we can see in the following snippet, in the first line of the snippet such devices are defined using the following code:

```
/* Declare all the needed pulse devices */
static struct {
        int gpio;
        char *name;
} pulse_data[] = {
        {
                .gpio = 67,
                .name = "oil",
        },
        {
                .gpio = 68,
                .name = "water",
        },
};
```

 The complete code is stored in the `chapter_05/pulse/pulse-bbb.c` file in the book's example code repository.

Here, we declare that the `oil` device is connected with the `gpio67` (**P8.8**) while the `water` one is connected with `gpio68` (**P8.10**).

In the `first_pulse_init()` function (which is executed when the module is first loaded into the kernel), we request the pulse devices by calling the `pulse_device_register()` function once per device. As an opposite action, during the module unloading (that is, when `first_pulse_exit()` is called), we release the allocated devices by calling the `pulse_device_unregister()` function once per device.

 Note that when we write the kernel code, we must release whatever we ask the kernel to, otherwise we'll lose it till the next reboot.

These two functions are implemented in the `pulse.c` file, as shown in the following code snippet:

```
struct pulse_device *pulse_device_register(char *name, int gpio)
{
        struct pulse_device *pdev;
```

```
        int ret;

        /* First allocate a new pulse device */
        pdev = kmalloc(sizeof(struct pulse_device), GFP_KERNEL);
        if (unlikely(!pdev))
                return ERR_PTR(-ENOMEM);

        /* Create the device abd init the device's data */
        pdev->dev = device_create(pulse_class, NULL, gpio, pdev, "%s", name);
        if (unlikely(IS_ERR(pdev->dev))) {
                dev_err(pdev->dev, "unable to create device %s at gpio %d\n",
                        name, gpio);
                ret = PTR_ERR(pdev->dev);
                goto error_device_create;
        }
        dev_set_drvdata(pdev->dev, pdev);
        pdev->dev->release = pulse_device_destruct;

        strncpy(pdev->name, name, PULSE_NAME_LEN);
        pdev->gpio = gpio;

        atomic_set(&pdev->counter, 0);
        pdev->old_status = -1;

        /* Then request GPIO */
        ret = gpio_request(gpio, pdev->name);
        if (ret) {
                dev_err(pdev->dev, "unable to request gpio %d\n", gpio);
                goto error_gpio_request;
        }
        gpio_direction_input(gpio);

        /* And as last task start the kernel timer */
        setup_timer(&pdev->ktimer, pulse_ktimer_event, (unsigned long) pdev);
        mod_timer(&pdev->ktimer, jiffies + KTIMER_FREQ);

        dev_info(pdev->dev, "pulse %s added on gpio%d\n",
                                        pdev->name, pdev->gpio);

        return pdev;

error_gpio_request:
        device_destroy(pulse_class, 0);

error_device_create:
        kfree(pdev);

        return ERR_PTR(ret);
}
```

```
EXPORT_SYMBOL(pulse_device_register);

void pulse_device_unregister(struct pulse_device *pdev)
{
        /* Drop all allocated resources */

        del_timer_sync(&pdev->ktimer);
        gpio_free(pdev->gpio);

        device_destroy(pulse_class, pdev->gpio);

        dev_info(pdev->dev, "pulse %s removed\n", pdev->name);
}
EXPORT_SYMBOL(pulse_device_unregister);
```

You can see all the steps done to create the driver data structures in the `register` function and the respective inverse steps done in the `unregister` one. Note that both the functions are declared as **exported symbols** by the code:

```
EXPORT_SYMBOL(pulse_device_register);
EXPORT_SYMBOL(pulse_device_unregister);
```

This tells the compiler that these functions are special, and they cannot be used by other kernel modules unless the functions are exported.

 This is another important concept that you should understand as-is, otherwise you can take a look the book *Linux Device Drivers, Third Edition* available at the bookshop and online at `http://lwn.net/Kernel/LDD3/`.

In the module initialization method (the `pulse_init()` function), we use the `class_create()` function to create our new pulse class, and as an opposite action, in the module exit (the `pulse_exit()` function), we will destroy it by calling `class_destroy()`.

You should now take a look at the `pulse_init()` function at line:

```
pulse_class->dev_groups = pulse_groups;
```

Using such an assignment, we will declare the four attribute files: `count`, `counter_and_reset`, `gpio`, and `set_to`, which are all reported in the `pulse_attrs` struct:

```
static struct attribute *pulse_attrs[] = {
        &dev_attr_gpio.attr,
        &dev_attr_counter.attr,
```

```
        &dev_attr_counter_and_reset.attr,
        &dev_attr_set_to.attr,
        NULL,
};
```

Each entry of the preceding structure is created by the DEVICE_ATTR_XX() function as follows:

```
static ssize_t gpio_show(struct device *dev,
        struct device_attribute *attr, char *buf)
{
    struct pulse_device *pdev = dev_get_drvdata(dev)

    return sprintf(buf, "%d\n", pdev->gpio);
}
static DEVICE_ATTR_RO(gpio);
```

This code specifies the attributes of the dev_attr_gpio.attr entry by declaring the file attribute gpio as read-only, and the gpio_show() function body is called each time from the user space when we do a read() system call on the file. In fact, as there are read() and write() system calls for files, similarly there are show() and store() functions for sysfs attributes.

As a dual example, the following code declares the attributes of the dev_attr_set_to.attr entry by declaring the set_to file attribute as write-only and the set_to_store() function body is called each time from the user space. We do a write() system call on the file:

```
static ssize_t set_to_store(struct device *dev,
                        struct device_attribute *attr,
                        const char *buf, size_t count)
{
        struct pulse_device *pdev = dev_get_drvdata(dev);
        int status, ret;

        ret = sscanf(buf, "%d", &status);
        if (ret != 1)
                return -EINVAL;

        atomic_set(&pdev->counter, status);

        return count;
}
static DEVICE_ATTR_WO(set_to);
```

> Note that the `sprintf()` and `sscanf()` functions, which are quite common functions for C programmers, are not the ones implemented in the libc, but they are homonym functions written ad hoc for the kernel space to simplify the kernel code development by representing well-known functions to the developer.

You should also notice that for the `show()` and `store()` functions, we have the following:

- The attribute files are the ones that get/set the data from/to the user space by reading/writing the data into the buffer pointed by the `buf` pointer.

- All these functions work on the `dev` pointer that represents the device, which is currently accessed that is, if the user gets access to the `oil` device, the `dev` pointer will point to a data structure, representing such a device. Remember what we said about the object-oriented programming. This magic allows the developer to write a clean and compact code.

The core of our driver is stored in the `pulse_device_register()` and `pulse_ktimer_event()` functions. As we can see, in the former function, we first create a new device according to the data passed:

```
/* Create the device abd init the device's data */
pdev->dev = device_create(pulse_class, NULL, gpio, pdev, "%s", name);
if (unlikely(IS_ERR(pdev->dev))) {
        dev_err(pdev->dev, "unable to create device %s at gpio %d\n",
                                                name, gpio);
        ret = PTR_ERR(pdev->dev);
        goto error_device_create;
}
```

Then, we request the needed GPIO line to the kernel and set it as an input line:

```
/* Then request GPIO */
ret = gpio_request(gpio, pdev->name);
if (ret) {
        dev_err(pdev->dev, "unable to request gpio %d\n", gpio);
        goto error_gpio_request;
}
gpio_direction_input(gpio);
```

> For more information on the functions used, you can refer to the appropriate section of the kernel source tree documentation directory in the `Documentation/gpio/gpio.txt` file.

In the end, we schedule a kernel timer, which in turn will call the `pulse_ktimer_event()` function:

```
/* And as last task start the kernel timer */
setup_timer(&pdev->ktimer, pulse_ktimer_event, (unsigned long) pdev);
mod_timer(&pdev->ktimer, jiffies + KTIMER_FREQ);
```

A kernel timer is a kernel mechanism used to schedule an event at a later time; in our code, we schedule the next event from now (the current value of the `jiffies` variable) plus `KTIMER_FREQ` (defined in the file at the beginning), which means that we'll schedule the event at 10 ms (1/100 seconds) in the future. When the kernel timer expires, the `pulse_ktimer_event()` function is called, which is shown as follows:

```
static void pulse_ktimer_event(unsigned long ptr)
{
        struct pulse_device *pdev = (struct pulse_device *) ptr;

        /* Get the gpio status */
        int status = !!gpio_get_value(pdev->gpio);

        /* Check for the first event  */
        if (pdev->old_status == -1) {
                pdev->old_status = status;
                goto end;
        }

        /* Check for the state changing and, in case, increment the counting */
        if (pdev->old_status != status) {
                pdev->old_status = status;
                atomic_inc(&pdev->counter);
        }

        end:
        /* Reschedule the kernel timer */
        mod_timer(&pdev->ktimer, jiffies + KTIMER_FREQ);
}
```

What we do in this function is quite clear: first, we get the GPIO status, then we check whether such a status has been changed, and in this case, we increment our counter. In the last step, we reschedule the kernel timer using the `mod_timer()` function (this is because the timer is already created, and we need to modify the expiring time only).

Note that this solution is far from the optimum; in fact, we should use interrupts instead of the kernel timers. However, again, this is out of the scope of this book, and so we decided to use the simplest solution to avoid the interrupts usage. Now to test the code, we should compile it, so let's use the following command:

`$ make KERNEL_DIR=../linux-dev/KERNEL/`

If everything works well, we should get the two kernel modules `pulse.ko` and `pulse-bbb.ko`, we defined in the `Makefile`.

> Note that `KERNEL_DIR` points to the directory where the kernel sources are, so you should set it accordingly to your system configuration.

Note that we just compiled the code against the kernel code that we rebuilt from scratch in the *Compiling the kernel* section of *Chapter 3, Compiling versus Cross-compiling*, that is, the kernel version 3.13.x, which we stored in the microSD. So, to load these kernel modules into our BeagleBone Black, we must use the distribution in the microSD. To be sure that we are running the right kernel, we can use the following command that shows the current kernel release:

```
root@BeagleBone:~# uname -a
Linux arm 3.13.10-bone9 #1 SMP Fri Nov 7 23:25:59 CET 2014 armv7l GNU/
Linux
```

> Of course, we can do the same on the distribution on the on-board eMMC, but in this case, we must compile the modules against the kernel version 3.8.x. To do so, we should first verify the kernel version on the eMMC on the BeagleBone Black:
>
> ```
> root@BeagleBone:~# uname -r
> 3.8.13-bone47
> ```
>
> Then, we should go to the directory where we downloaded the kernel sources into the host system and then retrieve the right kernel release using the following command:
>
> ```
> $ git checkout -b 3.8.13-bone47 3.8.13-bone47
> ```
>
> It may happen that we get an error like this:
>
> ```
> error: Your local changes to the following files would
> be overwritten by checkout:
>     build_kernel.sh
>     patches/defconfig
> Please, commit your changes or stash them before you can
> switch branches.
> Aborting
> ```
>
> In this case, we can fix it using the following command:
>
> ```
> $ git reset --hard
> ```

Then, we retry the checkout command:

```
$ git checkout -b 3.8.13-bone47 3.8.13-bone47
Switched to a new branch '3.8.13-bone47'
```

Then, we have to rebuild the kernel:

```
$ ./build_kernel.sh
```

When finished, the kernel tree is ready to be used to compile against the new kernel modules.

So, let's copy the two files to the BeagleBone Black (for instance, using the `scp` command), and then first, load the `pulse.ko` module with the following command:

**root@BeagleBone:~# insmod pulse.ko**

If we take a look at the kernel messages with `dmesg`, we should see the following message:

**Pulse driver support v. 0.50.0 - (C) 2014 Rodolfo Giometti**

Great! The new device class is now defined in the kernel; in fact, if we take a look at the `/sys/class/` **sysfs** directory, we can see that the new class is up and running:

**root@BeagleBone:~# ls -ld /sys/class/pulse/**

**drwxr-xr-x 2 root root 0 Jan  8 22:10 /sys/class/pulse/**

Now we should add the two devices `oil` and `water` defined in the `pulse-bbb.ko` module, so let's load it into the kernel:

**root@BeagleBone:~# insmod pulse-bbb.ko**

Again, using the `dmesg` command, we should see two new kernel messages:

**pulse oil: pulse oil added on gpio67**

**pulse water: pulse water added on gpio68**

This is what we expected! Now in the **sysfs**, we now have the following output:

**root@BeagleBone:~# ls -l /sys/class/pulse/**

**total 0**

**lrwxrwxrwx 1 root root 0 Jan  8 22:15 oil -> ../../devices/virtual/pulse/oil**

**lrwxrwxrwx 1 root root 0 Jan  8 22:15 water -> ../../devices/virtual/pulse/water**

Perfect! The system is now ready to count the pulses on the programmed GPIOs, but how can we generate these pulses to test the new driver? Well, this is quite simple, we can use the other two GPIOs as pulse generators and the script in the chapter_05/pulse_gen.sh file in the book's example code repository to actually generate the pulses.

We connect gpio65 (**P8.18**) to gpio67 (**P8.8**), and in another terminal window, we run the preceding script with the following command line:

```
root@BeagleBone:~# ./pulse_gen.sh 65 4
```

We generate a 4 Hz pulse signal from gpio65 (**P8.18**) to gpio67 (**P8.8**), where the oil counter is connected, so if we try to read its data, we get the following:

```
root@BeagleBone:~# cat /sys/class/pulse/oil/gpio
67
```

If we try to read the counter file, we can see that it increments at the speed of 4 pulses per second. However, the functioning may result more clear if we use the following commands that reset the counter first (using the set_to file), and then use the counter_and_reset file to restart the counting after each reading:

```
root@BeagleBone:~# echo 0 > /sys/class/pulse/oil/set_to ; while sleep 1 ;
do cat /sys/class/pulse/oil/counter_and_reset ; done
8
8
9
8
```

 Note that we get 8 instead of 4 because the pulse driver counts both high-to-low and low-to-high transactions. Also, note that 9 is due the fact that there can be some delays in reading the counting data.

Now the user can use another GPIO in order to play with the water counter.

# Summary

Now we know (more or less) what a device driver is, and how it can be easily implemented using the sysfs filesystem.

However, there exist tons of different device drivers for tons of computer peripherals, so starting from the next chapter, we'll see the most important computer peripherals available on the BeagleBone Black that an embedded developer may find in his/her professional life.

For each peripheral, we'll try to see how we can connect it to our BeagleBone Black, and how to configure and use the corresponding device driver by writing some example code. The next chapter talks about serial ports, which is one of the most important peripherals a computer can have.

# Serial Ports and TTY Devices

**6**

In the previous chapter, we saw how to manage an LED within the kernel using the sysfs API; however, this was just a really simple example of kernel programming used to show you how implementing a device driver can be trivial in simple cases. Unfortunately, this technique gets complex very quickly according to the peripheral complexity.

Starting from this chapter, we are going to look in detail at how several computer's peripherals can be connected to our BeagleBone Black, and how we can manage them in order to interact with the environment from the user space. That is, we are going to show you how you can get access to some peripherals by enabling and configuring the correct driver; in this case, we don't have to write a driver from scratch but knowing how a driver works, we can try to correctly use an already written one.

In this chapter, we will present the serial ports, one of the most important peripheral classes a computer can have (at least, a computer used in the control automation industry). After a brief description what a serial port or a serial device is, we'll see how we can manage them in a Linux system in order to use a real serial device.

## What is a serial port?

A **serial port** is not a peripheral, but it is a serial communication interface through which information transfers in or out one bit at a time. These interfaces are one of the most important communication ports we can have in an embedded device. In fact, in the first chapter, we discovered that we can get full control of our BeagleBone Black only by getting access to its serial console (which normally runs over a serial port even if, in our case, it has been emulated via a USB device).

In the industry market, we can find tons of peripherals that use a serial port to communicate with the CPU, so that's why we must know a bit more about how this communication interface works, and how we can get access to its connected devices in order to exchange data with them.

A peripheral using a serial port to communicate with the CPU is normally called a **serial peripheral** or **serial device**.

# The electrical lines

The serial port lines are mentioned in the following table:

| Name | Description |
|------|-------------|
| TxD — Transmitted Data | This carries data from DTE to DCE |
| RxD — Received Data | This carries data from DCE to DTE |
| DTR — Data Terminal Ready | This indicates the presence of DTE to DCE |
| DCD — Data Carrier Detect | This indicates that DCE is connected to the telephone line |
| DSR — Data Set Ready | This indicates that DCE is ready to receive commands or data |
| RI — Ring Indicator | This indicates that DCE has detected an incoming ring signal on the telephone line |
| RTS — Request To Send | This indicates that DTE requests the DCE to prepare to receive data |
| CTS — Clear To Send | This indicates that DCE is ready to accept data |

Note that most of the preceding lines are control ones and are not strictly required for a simple communication channel, so they can be left unconnected (recall what we did in the *Getting access to the serial console* section of *Chapter 2, Managing the System Console*, when we connect a serial adapter to the BeagleBone Black to get access to the serial console).

The required signals are TxD, RxD, and of course GND, so in our next examples, we will use these signals only.

According to the standard, the **DTE (Data Terminal Equipment)** is the device with the male connector, that is the PC, while the **DCE (Data Communication Equipment)** is the device with the female connector, that is, the controlled device.

You may get more information regarding these control lines on the Internet and a good starting point is at `http://en.wikipedia.org/wiki/Flow_control_%28data%29#Hardware_flow_control`.

# Implementation of serial ports

While interfaces, such as Ethernet or USB, send data as a serial stream, the term serial port usually identifies hardware compliant to the **RS-232** or **RS-422/RS-485** standard.

In modern computers, serial ports have been replaced by USB-to-serial devices because an RS-232 port can be easily emulated by a dedicated USB device (this is exactly what our BeagleBone Black does by default, as already seen in *The first login* section of *Chapter 1, Installing the Developing System*). However, the standard serial port's hardware still exists in the embedded and industrial world. The reason is quite simple: because the serial ports are easy to use and easy to implement (the hardware and software are light and do not engage the CPU too much). So, serial ports are still used in applications, such as industrial automation systems and remote monitoring or in some scientific instruments. It's quite easy to find industrial devices (not only a normal peripheral but just a complete system) that use one or more serial ports to communicate with other systems.

As already stated, the most used serial port implementations are the RS-232, RS-422, and RS-485. The RS-232 was so widely used that it had been used in every PC until USB devices made it obsolete, but it's still quite common to find a standard RS-232 port on an embedded computer nowadays.

The RS-422 and RS-485 implementations are still serial interfaces like the RS-232 implementation but with some electrical differences in order to allow communication between long distances, provide high noise immunity, and have multi-slave communication support.

> To explain all the serial port devices is beyond the scope of this book; however, first, you may take a look at http://en.wikipedia.org/wiki/Serial_port.
> In this book, we'll consider the RS-232 implementation only.

Another special case of serial ports that can be found on an embedded computer is the TTL **UART (Universal Asynchronous Receiver/Transmitter)**. These devices are integrated circuits designed to implement the interface for serial ports on PCs and embedded computers. While they are often connected to RS-232 (or 422/485) interfaces by proper hardware, they can be found as a raw connection to a TTL interface, too.

Serial communication at a **TTL (transistor-transistor logic)** level will always remain between the limits of GND and VCC, which is often 5 V or 3.3 V. A logic high (typically referred as 1) is represented by VCC, while a logic low (typically referred as 0) is GND.

This special case of a serial port is usually used for in-board serial communications, where the CPU communicates with a GPRS/GPS modem, several RFID readers, and so on, and in some cases, to exchange data with an external coprocessor or DSP.

# The serial ports in Linux

Despite all the preceding serial ports names, in GNU/Linux **/dev/ttyXXX**, where the *XXX* string may vary according to the specific serial port implementations. For instance, the historical (and standard) names of the PC's UART serial ports are /dev/ttyS0, /dev/ttyS1, and so on, but (as seen in the previous chapters) the USB-to-serial adapters can be named as /dev/ttyUSB0, /dev/ttyUSB1 or /dev/ttyACM0, /dev/ttyACM1, and so on.

The tty prefix comes from the very old abbreviation of teletypewriter and was originally associated only with the physical connection to a Unix system. Now that name also represents any serial port-style devices, such as serial ports, USB-to-serial converters, tty virtual devices, and so on.

The Linux **tty driver** core (that is implemented using a **char driver**) is responsible for controlling both the flow of data across a tty device and the format of the data. This is obtained using a **line discipline** (**LDISC**), which is a mid-layer between the upper layer (the device seen from the user space) and the lower hardware driver (the code that communicates with the hardware) that specifies how the data must be processed. For example, the standard line discipline processes the data it receives according to the requirements of a Unix terminal. So on input, it handles the special characters, such as the interrupt character (typically, *Ctrl + C*) and the erase and kill characters (typically, *Backspace* or *Delete*, and *Ctrl + U*, respectively), and on output, it replaces all the LF characters with a CR/LF sequence.

Because of this fact, we cannot simply open a tty device, and then start reading and writing data to it; in fact, the sent or received data will be modified by the current line discipline, so we must configure the tty device properly in order to get the right data flow. Typically, we want a clean data flow, and this mode can be achieved by setting the port in the raw mode.

In our example, we'll show you how to manage this situation.

# The communication parameters

Before we start to communicate with a serial device, we must know the communication parameters it uses, that is, which are the specific configuration settings of the serial data that we wish to transfer. So, we must know the speed, data bits, parity, and stop bits settings.

For the speed, only the fixed values are typically allowed; in fact, we must choose from 75, 110, 300, 1200, 2400, 4800, 9600, 19200, 38400, 57600, and 115200 bit/s.

In reality, other speed settings can be used. You should carefully read the datasheet of the serial device to check the allowed speeds. Regarding data bits, the usual setting is 8 (that is, 8 bits are used to transfer the information); we can even choose 6 (rarely used), 7 (for ASCII), 8, or 9 (rarely used). In the next examples, I'm going to use the value 8 for this setting.

Parity and stop bits are deeply related to the serial communication protocol, which I will not explain here, so you must forgive me if I don't spend many words on them. In the next example, I'm going to use the value None for parity and 1 for stop bits.

> You may get more information on parity and stop bits on the Internet and a good starting point is at http://en.wikipedia.org/wiki/Serial_port#Parity.

A concise way to represent the serial communication settings is, for instance, 115200,8N1, which means: *115200* bit/s, *8* data bits, *No* parity, and *1* stop bits.

Well, these communications settings are exactly the ones we will use in the next example.

# A simple serial echo

In order to explain a simple serial port communication, we can use the code stored in the chapter_06/echo.py file in the book's example code repository on our host PC, as a serial device that echos the serial data received from the BeagleBone Black.

The code is quite self-explanatory; however, we should note that the serial parameters are set during the communication channel created with the following code:

```
# Configure the serial connections
ser = serial.Serial(
        port        = dev,
        baudrate    = 115200,
        bytesize    = 8,
        parity      = 'N',
        stopbits    = 1,
        timeout     = None,
        xonxoff     = 0,
        rtscts      = 0
)
```

While the main server and client functionalities are covered in the homonym-named functions `server()` and `client()`.

You will notice that this program can work in both server or client mode just by using the correct command line:

```
root@BeagleBone:~# ./echo.py -h
usage:  echo.py  [-h] client|server <serdev>
```

So, for instance, if we wish to run the program in server mode on the /dev/ttyUSB0 serial port, we should use the following command line:

```
$ ./echo.py -h server /dev/ttyUSB0
```

Now we only need a serial connection to test our code.

In *The first login* section of *Chapter 1, Installing the Developing System*, we saw how we can get connected to the BeagleBone Black from the host PC through the /dev/ACM0 device, so we can use this device to send and receive the serial data. For instance, we can choose to run the preceding echo server on the host PC and the client on the BeagleBone Black, but before we proceed, it's better to disable the default serial terminal that also runs by default on the /dev/ttyACM0 device; otherwise, it can interfere with the echo server. To do so, we should use the following command:

```
root@BeagleBone:~# systemctl stop getty@ttyGS0.service
```

Now if we try to run a minicom session on the /dev/ttyACM0 device on our host PC, we should get no prompt at all. To double-check this, we can verify that on the BeagleBone Black, the getty program does not use the /dev/ttyGS0 device anymore with the following command:

```
root@BeagleBone:~# fuser -v /dev/ttyGS0
```

If no output is displayed, then we can successfully disable the serial console; otherwise, if we get an output like the following, this means that something went wrong:

```
root@BeagleBone:~# fuser -v /dev/ttyGS0
                     USER       PID ACCESS COMMAND
/dev/ttyGS0:         root      1935 F.... agetty
```

The /dev/ttyGS0 device is the corresponding device of /dev/ttyACM0 that is managed by the g_multi USB gadget driver (see the *Acting as a device* section of *Chapter 7, Universal Serial Bus – USB*, for further information).

The getty program is the one that the system uses to manage user login.

Well, now on the host PC, we can safely run the following command in order to start the serial echo server:

```
$ ./echo.py server /dev/ttyACM0
```

While on the BeagleBone Black, we run the following command:

```
root@BeagleBone:~# ./echo.py client /dev/ttyGS0
>>
```

If we now try to enter the Test line string followed by the *Enter* key on the client, we should get an output as follows:

```
root@BeagleBone:~# ./echo.py client /dev/ttyGS0
>> Test line
got:  Test line
```

While on the server, we get the following output:

```
$ ./echo.py server /dev/ttyACM0
echoing:  Test line
```

Now we can continue to enter more lines until, using the exit string, we close the communication:

```
root@BeagleBone:~# ./echo.py client /dev/ttyGS0
>> Test line
got:  Test line
>> Second line
got:  Second line
>> another one...
got:  another one...
>> exit
root@BeagleBone:~#
```

If we take a look at the server's output, we get the following:

```
src/serial$ ./echo.py server /dev/ttyACM0
echoing:  Test line
echoing:  Second line
echoing:  another one...
echoing:  exit
```

To stop the server, just use the *Ctrl* + *C* keys.

# Managing a real device

Echoing data over an emulated serial connection can be educational, but we want to manage real devices, so let's connect one to our BeagleBone Black.

The BeagleBone Black has six on-board serial ports but only one is enabled by default: the /dev/ttyO0 device that is coupled to the serial console, as we saw in the previous chapters. The other serial ports must be enabled before they can be used.

 The default serial port name for the BeagleBone Black is **/dev/ttyOX**, where *X* addresses the *X*-th available serial port.

If we do log in to the system, we can easily verify this using the following command:

```
root@BeagleBone:~# ls -l /dev/ttyO*
crw-rw---- 1 root tty 248, 0 Apr 23 20:20 /dev/ttyO0
```

Ok, the /dev/ttyO0 device is the only available serial port.

To enable the other serial ports, we need to modify the kernel settings in order to ask it to enable the serial port we wish to use. Which ports need to be enabled depends on the pins we'd like to use to connect our device. The following table may help us in choosing them:

| Device | TxD | RxD | RTS | CTS | Name |
|---|---|---|---|---|---|
| /dev/ttyO1 | P9.24 | P9.26 | | | **UART1** |
| /dev/ttyO2 | P9.21 | P9.22 | P8.38 | P8.37 | **UART2** |
| /dev/ttyO4 | P9.13 | P9.11 | P8.33 | P8.35 | **UART4** |
| /dev/ttyO5 | P8.37 | P8.38 | | | **UART5** |

> You should remember that the notation **P9.26** means that pin **26** is on the expansion connector **P9**.
>
> We can get these values directly from the BeagleBone Black firmware settings using the following command:
>
> ```
> root@BeagleBone:~# dtc -I dtb -O dts <dtbo>
> ```
>
>  Here, <dtbo> is one of the firmware files available in the `/lib/firmware/` directory:
>
> ```
> root@BeagleBone:~# ls /lib/firmware/BB-UART*.dtbo
> /lib/firmware/BB-UART1-00A0.dtbo
> /lib/firmware/BB-UART2-00A0.dtbo
> /lib/firmware/BB-UART2-RTSCTS-00A0.dtbo
> /lib/firmware/BB-UART4-00A0.dtbo
> /lib/firmware/BB-UART4-RTSCTS-00A0.dtbo
> /lib/firmware/BB-UART5-00A0.dtbo
> ```

All the devices are used for our scope, so I choose to use the /dev/ttyO2 device. In order to activate the serial port /dev/ttyO2, we can use the following command:

```
root@BeagleBone:~# echo BB-UART2 > /sys/devices/bone_capemgr.9/slots
```

On the serial console, we should see the following activity:

```
bone-capemgr bone_capemgr.9: part_number 'BB-UART2', version 'N/A'
bone-capemgr bone_capemgr.9: slot #7: generic override
bone-capemgr bone_capemgr.9: bone: Using override eeprom data at
slot 7
bone-capemgr bone_capemgr.9: slot #7: 'Override Board Name,00A0,Override
Manuf,BB-UART2'
bone-capemgr bone_capemgr.9: slot #7: Requesting part number/version
based 'BB-UART2-00A0.dtbo
bone-capemgr bone_capemgr.9: slot #7: Requesting firmware 'BB-UART2-00A0.
dtbo' for board-name 'Override Board Name', version '00A0'
bone-capemgr bone_capemgr.9: slot #7: dtbo 'BB-UART2-00A0.dtbo' loaded;
converting to live tree
bone-capemgr bone_capemgr.9: slot #7: #2 overlays 48024000.serial: ttyO2
at MMIO 0x48024000 (irq = 74) is a OMAP UART2
bone-capemgr bone_capemgr.9: slot #7: Applied #2 overlays.
```

Now the /dev/ttyO2 device should be available:

```
root@BeagleBone:~# ls -l /dev/ttyO*
crw------- 1 root tty     248, 0 Apr 23 23:21 /dev/ttyO0
crw-rw---T 1 root dialout 248, 2 Apr 23 23:20 /dev/ttyO2
```

Now on a serial device, we can use the following RFID LF reader that sends its data through a serial port at TTL 3.3 V level:

 The device can be purchased at `http://www.cosino.io/`
`product/lf-rfid-low-voltage-reader` or elsewhere
on the Internet.

It can be directly connected to our BeagleBone Black at the following pins of the expansion connector **P9**:

| BeagleBone Black pins – label | RFID LF reader pins – label |
|---|---|
| 4 – VCC | 8 – VCC |
| 22 – RxD | 6 – TX |
| 2 – GND | 7 – GND |

After all the pins have been connected, the tags data will be available at the /dev/tty02 device, and in order to quickly verify this, we can use the following commands:

```
root@BeagleBone:~# stty -F /dev/ttyO2 9600 raw
root@BeagleBone:~# cat /dev/ttyO2
```

Then, when we approach a tag, we should hear a beep and the corresponding tag's ID should appear on the command line as follows:

```
root@BeagleBone:~# cat /dev/ttyO2
.6F007F4E1E40
```

The `stty` command is a standard tool used to manage the serial devices settings. Using this command, we set a speed of 9600 bits/s and the raw mode for the `/dev/ttyO2` device.

You can get more information on this by taking a look at its man pages using the following command:

```
$ man stty
```

Hence, it is quite easy to properly filter the bytes in order to display the tag's ID only, and you will find a possible implementation in the `chapter_06/echo.py` file in the book's example code repository. To execute it, we have to use the following command line:

**root@BeagleBone:~# ./rfid_lf.py /dev/ttyO2**

**6F007F4E1E40**

**6F007F48C199**

To get the preceding output, we simply need to approach the RFID LF tags. In fact, each time the RFID reader detects a tag, it sends its data through the serial port, and the program gets the data with the `read()` function, as shown in the following snippet:

```
def reader(ser):
        while True:
                line = ser.readline()
                line = filter(lambda x: x in string.printable, line)
                print(line.replace("\n", "")),
```

The function is really simple; in fact, the `ser.realined()` function gets the tag data, the `filter()` function does some filtering actions to get human-readable characters, while the `print()` function displays the results.

# Summary

Serial ports and serial devices are one of the most important concepts of an embedded computer but tons of other peripherals exist. You should try to modify the preceding example programs in order to fit your needs, or you can go directly to the next sections, where we'll introduce you to some new devices.

In the next chapter, we will take a look at the **Universal Serial Bus (USB)** that allows people to connect several kinds of electronic devices to a computer through the same port: for instance, a hard disk, a keyboard, or a serial device, as seen in this chapter.

# 7
# Universal Serial Bus – USB

Now it's time to take a look at **Universal Serial Bus (USB)**, a versatile bus widely used in modern PCs that allows people to connect an electronic device to a computer, for instance, a hard disk, a keyboard, or a serial device (as seen in the previous chapter) can all be connected to a computer through the same USB port.

After a brief introduction about what this bus is and how it works, we'll show you the different types of USB devices and how they are supported in the BeagleBone Black's kernel. The BeagleBone Black can act as a USB host in order to manage a barcode reader; then we will see how we can use the BeagleBone Black as a USB device in order to exchange data with a host PC.

## What is the Universal Serial Bus?

The **Universal Serial Bus** is a computer bus used by a CPU and its peripherals to communicate with each other. In every USB communication, at least one USB host and one USB device exists. The former is the one that effectively directs the traffic flow to the devices, while the latter is the one that simply answers all the host's requests.

Practically, the USB host periodically queries all the connected USB devices in order to discover whether they want to send a message to it.

So, the host is smart enough to understand what kind of peripheral the user has connected to, and it can reconfigure the system in order to correctly manage it. This magic happens each time a USB device is first connected to a USB host, thanks to the enumeration process.

The enumeration starts by sending a reset signal to the USB device (at this stage, the data rate of the USB device is also automatically determined), and after the reset, all the information of the USB device is read by the host, and the peripheral device is unequivocally identified.

At this stage, if the system has a proper device driver to manage the peripheral, it will load the driver, and the device is set to a *configured state*. If the USB host is restarted, the enumeration process is repeated for all the connected devices.

 Let me suggest that you get more information on USB internals on the Internet; a good starting point would be http://simple. wikipedia.org/wiki/Universal_Serial_Bus.

For instance, if we connect a USB keyboard to our BeagleBone Black, and we monitor the kernel messages, we should see something like this:

```
usb usb1: usb wakeup-resume
usb usb1: usb auto-resume
hub 1-0:1.0: hub_resume
hub 1-0:1.0: port 1: status 0301 change 0001
hub 1-0:1.0: state 7 ports 1 chg 0002 evt 0000
hub 1-0:1.0: port 1, status 0301, change 0000, 1.5 Mb/s
usb 1-1: new low-speed USB device number 2 using musb-hdrc
```

Here, the enumeration process ends when the device number 2 is assigned to the new device. Then, the system continues with reading the information of the new device:

```
usb 1-1: skipped 1 descriptor after interface
usb 1-1: udev 2, busnum 1, minor = 1
usb 1-1: New USB device found, idVendor=04d9, idProduct=1203
usb 1-1: New USB device strings: Mfr=0, Product=0, SerialNumber=0
usb 1-1: usb_probe_device
usb 1-1: configuration #1 chosen from 1 choice
usb 1-1: adding 1-1:1.0 (config #1, interface 0)
```

At this point, the host has read all the information, and has set the device configuration. In particular, we should notice the vendor ID (idVendor) and the product ID (idProduct) numbers. These numbers specify the device functions in the kernel.

Now, the kernel has all it needs to try and load a proper device driver; in fact, in the kernel messages, we see the following:

```
usbhid 1-1:1.0: usb_probe_interface
usbhid 1-1:1.0: usb_probe_interface - got id
```

```
input: HID 04d9:1203 as /devices/ocp.3/47400000.usb/musb-hdrc.1.auto/
usb1/1-1/1-1:1.0/input/input1
```

```
hid-generic 0003:04D9:1203.0001: input,hidraw0: USB HID v1.11 Keyboard
[HID 04d9:1203] on usb-musb-hdrc.1.auto-1/input0
```

```
usb 1-1: adding 1-1:1.1 (config #1, interface 1)
```

```
usbhid 1-1:1.1: usb_probe_interface
```

```
usbhid 1-1:1.1: usb_probe_interface - got id
```

```
input: HID 04d9:1203 as /devices/ocp.3/47400000.usb/musb-hdrc.1.auto/
usb1/1-1/1-1:1.1/input/input2
```

```
hid-generic 0003:04D9:1203.0002: input,hidraw1: USB HID v1.11 Device [HID
04d9:1203] on usb-musb-hdrc.1.auto-1/input1
```

```
hub 1-0:1.0: state 7 ports 1 chg 0000 evt 0002
```

```
hub 1-0:1.0: port 1 enable change, status 00000303
```

Ok, after this stage, the input driver is loaded, which manages a keyboard.

# The electrical lines

The USB port lines are reported in the following table:

| Name | Description |
| --- | --- |
| D+ | Data positive |
| D- | Data negative |
| VCC | Power line at 5 V |
| GND | Common ground |

Note that the preceding table refers to USB 1.1 and USB 2.0 standards only, since USB 3.x, more signals have been added.

As a special feature, the USB bus includes the VCC signal too; this is because it can power the devices directly from the bus.

# The USB bus in Linux

As already stated, both the USB host and USB device exist, and the same is valid for the Linux kernel, where we can find dedicated device drivers for both types. The only difference is that, in the kernel, the USB devices are named USB gadgets to avoid misunderstanding the typical meaning of the word *device*.

The USB hosts are all those devices that act as a master in a USB communication. Typically, a PC acts as a master, but an embedded computer can act as a USB gadget too. If you remember what we saw in *The first login* section of *Chapter 1, Installing the Developing System*, where we described how to boot for the first time, the BeagleBone Black was the USB gadget, while the host PC was the USB host.

The USB communication is very simple: there is a master that polls the various peripheral devices. This poll is done using several channels called **endpoints**, which can carry data in one direction only, either from the host computer to the device (so, the endpoint is called an **OUT** endpoint) or from the device to the host computer (so, the endpoint is called an **IN** endpoint).

Along with the direction, a USB endpoint can be also classified by considering how the data is transmitted by it. So, there exists four different endpoint types:

- **Control**: Control endpoints are commonly used for configuring the device and/or retrieving information about the device. Every USB device must have a control endpoint called **endpoint 0**, which is used by the USB subsystem to configure the device as soon as it has been inserted into the system.

  These endpoints are used for asynchronous data transfers.

- **Interrupt**: Interrupt endpoints are used to emulate the interrupt lines that we can find in every CPU. It can transfer small amounts of data at a fixed rate every time the USB host asks the device for the data. Due their specific tasks, these transfers are guaranteed by the USB protocol to always have enough reserved bandwidth to make it through.

  These endpoints are used for synchronous data transfers.

- **Bulk**: Bulk endpoints are used to transfer large amounts of data (a lot more than interrupt endpoints), and they are very common for devices that need to transfer any data that must get through with no data loss, but with no guarantee by the USB protocol to always make it through in a specific amount of time.

  These endpoints used for asynchronous data transfers are definitely not suitable for real-time data, such as audio and video devices, but they are used in printers, storage, and network devices.

- **Isochronous**: Isochronous endpoints exist to fill the gap left by the bulk endpoints and have the ability to transfer large amounts of data in real time - that is, data loss may happen, and only a transfer time is guaranteed.

  These endpoints used for synchronous data transfers are common in audio and video devices.

# Acting as a host

Our BeagleBone Black board has a USB host port; so, of course, it can act as a host. There is nothing special to do here since the proper driver is already up and running in the BeagleBone Black's default kernel configuration. We can have several possibilities: we can use the USB keys or external hard disks as storage devices, or we can use a USB-to-serial converter (as we did with our host PC to get connected to the BeagleBone Black's serial console). We can also use a USB keyboard or mouse as an input device, or a USB Wi-Fi dongle, and so on. (the list can be very long!).

As a real, simple, and educational example, we will see how to use a USB barcode reader with the BeagleBone Black.

There exist many of these device classes and all of them work in the same manner. However, we have to choose one, so we will use this device:

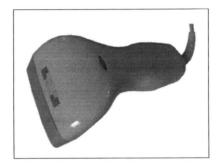

 The device can be purchased at (or by surfing the Internet) http://www.cosino.io/product/usb-barcode-reader.

This device class simply acts as a normal USB keyboard. In fact, the result of using this device is that the string corresponding to the read barcode ID appears in the system, as if it was inserted through a keyboard. Ok, it's simpler to show how it works than explaining it.

When we connect you to the BeagleBone Black, we should see something like this in the kernel messages:

```
usb 1-1: configuration #1 chosen from 1 choice
usb 1-1: adding 1-1:1.0 (config #1, interface 0)
usbhid 1-1:1.0: usb_probe_interface
usbhid 1-1:1.0: usb_probe_interface - got id
```

```
input: USBPS2 as /devices/ocp.3/47400000.usb/musb-hdrc.1.auto/usb1/1-1/1-
1:1.0/input/input1
```

```
hid-generic 0003:0D3D:0001.0001: input,hidraw0: USB HID v1.00 Keyboard
[USBPS2] on usb-musb-hdrc.1.auto-1/input0
```

```
usb 1-1: adding 1-1:1.1 (config #1, interface 1)
```

```
usbhid 1-1:1.1: usb_probe_interface
```

```
usbhid 1-1:1.1: usb_probe_interface - got id
```

```
input: USBPS2 as /devices/ocp.3/47400000.usb/musb-hdrc.1.auto/usb1/1-1/1-
1:1.0/input/input1
```

>  Note that the output may differ a bit even if we use the same device. In this example, there exists different versions of the same reader.

As we can see, the system thinks that a keyboard has been connected, and as reported in the kernel messages, the new input device `input1` should appear in the /sys/class/input directory:

```
root@BeagleBone:~# ls /sys/class/input/input1/
capabilities   event1   modalias   phys    properties   uevent
device         id       name       power   subsystem    uniq
```

>  If after plugging in the device, we do not see any of the preceding messages, we may have a buggy kernel. A USB barcode reader is already inserted:
>
> root@BeagleBone:~# cat /dev/bus/usb/001/001 > /dev/null
>
> Then, the device should now appear.

Ok, the device is up and running. Now, to test it, we use the code stored in the chapter_07/key_read.py file in the book's example code repository. This program uses the Python evdev library that can be installed using the following command line:

```
root@BeagleBone:~# pip install evdev
Downloading/unpacking evdev
  Downloading evdev-0.4.6.tar.gz
  Running setup.py egg_info for package evdev


Installing collected packages: evdev
  Running setup.py install for evdev
```

```
   building 'evdev._input' extension

   gcc -pthread -fno-strict-aliasing -DNDEBUG -g -fwrapv -O2
-Wall -Wstrict-prototypes -fPIC -I/usr/include/python2.7 -c evdev/
input.c -o build/temp.linux-armv7l-2.7/evdev/input.o -std=c99 -Wno-
error=declaration-after-statement

...

Successfully installed evdev
```

Cleaning up! This program is really simple, and the most interesting aspect of it is where we use the `evdev` library to read the data. A snippet of the code is reported as follows:

```python
# Now read data from the input device printing only letters and numbers
# Try to open the input device
try:
        dev = InputDevice(args[0])
except:
        print("invalid input device", args[0], file=sys.stderr)
        sys.exit(1);

# Now read data from the input device printing only letters and numbers
while True:
        r, w, x = select([dev], [], [])
        for event in dev.read():
                # Print key pressed events only
                if event.type == ecodes.EV_KEY and event.value == 1:
                        print(keys[event.code], end = "")
                        sys.stdout.flush()       # needed by print()
```

Using the `InputDevice()` function, we get an input device handler of the device passed by the user, and then we wait for an input event (`EV_KEY`) with the `select()` function; when it arrives, we read and decode it, and, in the end, we just print its data using the `keys` lookup table.

If we run the program using the following command, we can read a barcode image as follows:

```
root@BeagleBone:~# ./key_read.py /dev/input/event1
.test..barcode.
```

In the preceding example, the following barcode has been used:

Test Barcode

Note that you should press *Ctrl + C* keys to kill the process.

# Acting as a device

A very interesting functionality that a GNU/Linux embedded system can offer is the possibility to act as a USB device using the USB gadget subsystem. This permits us to use our embedded system as, for example, a USB key to store a complete filesystem, or allow a serial/Ethernet communication between another PC over a normal USB cable, and so on.

In *The first login* section of *Chapter 1, Installing the Developing System*, we already used the USB serial communication in order to get connected to the Linux's serial console; in this case, we used the serial port of the multi gadget (that is, the /dev/ACM0 device). In *The SSH tools* section of *Chapter 1, Installing the Developing System*, we had already used the Ethernet port of the multi gadget (that is, the usb0 device) in order to transfer some files from the host PC to our BeagleBone Black through an Ethernet connection.

However, a third device is available in the multi gadget device: a USB storage. So, now it's the time to see how we can use this device to exchange data with the host PC.

Several gadget devices are available in the system, and we cannot present all of them in this book. However, you can take a look at the /lib/modules/$(uname -r)/kernel/drivers/usb/gadget directory on the running BeagleBone Black kernel in order to discover the available gadget modules:

```
root@BeagleBone:~# ls /lib/modules/$(uname -r)/kernel/drivers/usb/gadget/
g_acm_ms.ko  g_ffs.ko           g_multi.ko     g_serial.ko  libcomposite.ko
g_audio.ko   g_hid.ko           g_ncm.ko       g_webcam.ko
g_cdc.ko     g_mass_storage.ko  g_nokia.ko     g_zero.ko
g_ether.ko   g_midi.ko          g_printer.ko   gadgetfs.ko
```

Then, you can take a look at the *Linux-USB Gadget API Framework* at the URL http://www.linux-usb.org/gadget/ (the guide is a bit outdated, but it still remains a good starting point).

First of all, we must be able to unload the default `g_multi` gadget driver that is loaded at boot since we need to reconfigure it. We can verify that `g_multi` is already running using the `lsmod` command to list all the currently loaded modules:

```
root@BeagleBone:~# lsmod
Module                  Size  Used by
g_multi                47670  2
libcomposite           14299  1 g_multi
mt7601Usta            601404  0
```

Now, to be able to unload the `g_multi` module, we must discover who is using it and make sure that the `Used by` value is not set to 0. In fact, if we try to unload the module, we get the following output:

```
root@BeagleBone:~# modprobe -r g_multi
FATAL: Module g_multi is in use.
```

A possible solution is to use the `fuser` command that shows all the processes that currently use a file:

```
root@BeagleBone:~# fuser -v /dev/ttyGS0
                        USER        PID ACCESS COMMAND
/dev/ttyGS0:            root       1658 F....  agetty
```

> Note that this procedure must be executed from the serial console, otherwise both the `usb0` and `/dev/ttyACM0` devices will disappear after the `g_multi` gadget driver is unloaded.

So, we have to stop `agetty` to unlock the `g_multi` module; this can be done by stopping a service put up by the system daemon **systemd**:

```
root@BeagleBone:~# systemctl stop serial-getty@ttyGS0.service
root@BeagleBone:~# modprobe -r g_multi
root@BeagleBone:~# lsmod
Module                  Size  Used by
mt7601Usta            601404  0
```

The **systemd** is a suite of system management and utilities designed to replace the Linux **init** system (the first process is executed in the user space during the Linux start up process). The BeagleBone Black's on-board Debian distribution uses this, and you may get more information on systemd on the Internet at `http://en.wikipedia.org/wiki/Systemd`.

Ok, now we can create a new file that will represent our USB storage. Using the following command line, we can create a zero filled file of 64 MB size:

```
root@BeagleBone:~# dd if=/dev/zero of=/opt/mass_storage bs=1M count=64
64+0 records in
64+0 records out
67108864 bytes (67 MB) copied, 2.53325 s, 26.5 MB/s
```

Now everything is in place, just reload the `g_multi` driver with the following command line that tells the kernel that the storage file is now the one we just created:

```
root@BeagleBone:~# modprobe g_multi file=/opt/mass_storage ro=0
```

After executing the preceding command, we should see something like this on the host PC kernel messages:

```
usb 2-1.4.3.4: new high-speed USB device number 75 using ehci-pci

usb 2-1.4.3.4: New USB device found, idVendor=1d6b, idProduct=0104

usb 2-1.4.3.4: New USB device strings: Mfr=2, Product=3, SerialNumber=0

usb 2-1.4.3.4: Product: Multifunction Composite Gadget

usb 2-1.4.3.4: Manufacturer: Linux 3.8.13-bone47 with musb-hdrc

rndis_host 2-1.4.3.4:1.0 usb0: register 'rndis_host' at usb-0000:00:1d.0-1.4.3.4,
RNDIS device, 0a:8b:45:05:fb:68

cdc_acm 2-1.4.3.4:1.2: This device cannot do calls on its own. It is not a modem.

cdc_acm 2-1.4.3.4:1.2: ttyACM0: USB ACM device

usb-storage 2-1.4.3.4:1.4: USB Mass Storage device detected

scsi18 : usb-storage 2-1.4.3.4:1.4

scsi 18:0:0:0: Direct-Access     Linux    File-CD Gadget   0308 PQ: 0 ANSI: 2

sd 18:0:0:0: Attached scsi generic sg2 type 0

sd 18:0:0:0: [sdb] 131072 512-byte logical blocks: (67.1 MB/64.0 MiB)

sd 18:0:0:0: [sdb] Write Protect is off

sd 18:0:0:0: [sdb] Mode Sense: 0f 00 00 00

sd 18:0:0:0: [sdb] Write cache: enabled, read cache: enabled, doesn't support DPO
or FUA

sdb: unknown partition table

sd 18:0:0:0: [sdb] Attached SCSI disk
```

As we can see in the preceding code, the host PC has found a 64 MB disk with an invalid partition table. It is quite obvious that the device is filled with zeros.

So, we just need to format the new disk by creating a FAT disk on the BeagleBone Black:

```
# mkfs.vfat -i BBB -I /dev/sdb
mkfs.fat 3.0.26 (2014-03-07)
```

Now, to test the new storage device, we can mount it, and then write a test file on it:

```
$ echo TEST_PC > /media/giometti/0000-0BBB/file_pc.txt
$ ls /media/giometti/0000-0BBB/
file_pc.txt
```

> Mounting and unmounting the device on the host PC depends on the distribution used, and on my Ubuntu, I just clicked on the respective icon to do this. However, let me remind you that, in case your host system has no automount features, you can use the mount command to do it manually.

Now we can unmount the disk, and then mount it on the BeagleBone Black filesystem in order to reread the preceding file:

```
root@BeagleBone:~# mount -o loop /opt/mass_storage /mnt/
root@BeagleBone:~# ls /mnt/
file_pc.txt
root@BeagleBone:~# cat /mnt/file_pc.txt
TEST_PC
```

A dual action can now be done within the BeagleBone Black by creating another file with the following command:

```
root@BeagleBone:~# echo TEST_BBB > /mnt/file_bbb.txt
```

Now, the disk can be unmounted and then remounted on the host PC in order to verify that the new file is present.

# Accessing the raw bus

In some circumstances, it can happen that a USB device lacks a dedicated device driver; in this case, a GNU/Linux system simply enumerates it, and then no driver is loaded at all. In this situation, the user cannot get access to the new USB device in any manner, except by accessing it using the raw commands directly over the bus. Simply speaking, it directly sends the USB messages to the new device and then manages the answers without using any dedicated driver at all.

You should note that if this new device has no available driver, then it cannot be seen from the system as any usual device (for example, a keyboard or a storage disk), so we have no `/dev/event2` or `/dev/sdb` entries to use. However, even if this situation may appear quite strange and difficult, in reality, it's not so terrible. In fact, for very simple devices, we can implement a simple management code in the user space using the `libusb` library on the host PC.

We can use the `libusb` library on the BeagleBone Black too if we decide to use it as a USB host and attach a device to the BeagleBone Black and be able to control it.

As a simple demonstration of how to use this technique, let me show you the following example that runs on the host PC, which acts as a USB host and uses the USB gadget driver `g_zero` on our BeagleBone Black, acting as a USB gadget. This particular device has two bulk endpoints: one for the input and one for the output, which can receive and send special messages respectively when requested.

As before, we can test the following procedure from the serial console only, as both the `usb0` and `/dev/ttyACM0` devices will disappear just after the `g_multi` gadget driver is unloaded.

Well, let's see how we can interact with this special gadget from the user space. To do this, we must unload the `g_multi` driver, as before, and then load the `g_zero` driver with the following command line:

```
root@BeagleBone:~# modprobe g_zero
```

It may happen that after the module has loaded, we get the following kernel message:

```
musb_g_ep0_irq 710: SetupEnd came in a wrong ep0stage setup
```

If so, just unload the module with the following command:

```
root@BeagleBone:~# modprobe -r g_zero
```

Then, try to reload it as before until no error messages are displayed.

On the host PC should now disappear all the USB devices managed by the
g_multi driver and a new device should be on the scene; in fact, if we take
a look at the host PC kernel messages, we should see the following:

```
usbtest 2-1.4:2.0: Linux gadget zero
usbtest 2-1.4:2.0: high-speed {control in/out bulk-in bulk-out} tests (+alt)
```

Using the lsusb command, we can read its vendor and product IDs, as shown in
the following command line:

```
$ lsusb | grep 'Gadget Zero'
Bus 002 Device 039: ID 0525:a4a0 Netchip Technology, Inc. Linux-USB "Gadget Zero"
```

So, by running the lsusb command again, and specifying the preceding values, we
can get more information on the g_zero device:

```
# lsusb -v -d 0525:a4a0
Bus 002 Device 036: ID 0525:a4a0 Netchip Technology, Inc. Linux-USB
"Gadget Zero"
Device Descriptor:
  bLength                 18
  bDescriptorType          1
  bcdUSB                2.00
  bDeviceClass           255 Vendor Specific Class
  bDeviceSubClass          0
  bDeviceProtocol          0
  bMaxPacketSize0         64
  idVendor            0x0525 Netchip Technology, Inc.
  idProduct           0xa4a0 Linux-USB "Gadget Zero"
  bcdDevice             3.08
  iManufacturer            1 Linux 3.8.13-bone47 with musb-hdrc
  iProduct                 2 Gadget Zero
  iSerial                  3 0123456789.0123456789.0123456789
  bNumConfigurations       2
```

Ok, the gadget is connected to the host PC, so let's move on and compile the testing
code in the chapter_07/usb_se ndrecv/usb_sendrecv.c file in the book's example
code repository. However, we need the libusb package to compile it, so let's install
the package with the following command:

```
$ sudo aptitude install libusb-dev
```

Now, we can compile the code using the usual `make` command as well. If we take a look at the following code snippet, we can see that after initializing the library, with the `libusb_init()` function, we open the device using the `libusb_open_device_with_vid_pid()` function with the proper vendor (VENDOR_ID) and product IDs (PRODUCT_ID) for the `g_zero` gadget. Then, after claiming the device's interface 0, we start the data bulk transfers using the `libusb_bulk_transfer()` function:

```
/* Send an all-zeros message to endpoint 0x01 */
ret = libusb_bulk_transfer(handle, 0x01, buffer,
                                sizeof(buffer), &n, 100);
if (ret) {
    fprintf(stderr, "error sending message to device ret=%d\n",
                    ret);
    exit(-1);
}
printf("%d bytes transmitted successfully\n", n);


/* Receive an all-zeros message from endpoint 0x81 */
ret = libusb_bulk_transfer(handle, 0x81, buffer,
                                sizeof(buffer), &n, 100);
if (ret) {
    fprintf(stderr, "error receiving message from device ret=%d\n",
                    ret);
        exit(-1);
}
if (n != sizeof(buffer)) {
    fprintf(stderr, "error receiving %d bytes while expecting %d\n",
                        n, sizeof(buffer));
        exit(-1);
}
printf("%d bytes received successfully\n", n);
```

> Note that the USB device interfaces are not covered in this book (see the *USB specifications* for detailed information). However, you should know that using such interfaces, we can create a composite device, such as the BeagleBone Black itself, that exposes the serial interface, mass storage device, and network interface all on the same device.

In the preceding code, we should also notice that in the first call of `libusb_bulk_transfer()`, we send an all-zero message to the BeagleBone Black through the endpoint `0x01`, which is the OUT endpoint; then with the same function, we receive an all-zeros message from the BeagleBone Black through the endpoint `0x81`, which is the IN endpoint.

Now we can test the communication with the `g_zero` gadget driver from the user space by running the program, as shown in the following command line:

```
$ sudo ./usb_sendrecv
g_zero device found
512 bytes transmitted successfully
512 bytes received successfully
```

> Note that we need the `sudo` command in order to run the program as a privileged user since, by default, the raw access to the bus is not allowed to a normal user. However, this behavior can be changed by writing a proper **udev** rule, but this topic is out of the scope of this book.

# Summary

The USB has become the ubiquitous standard for peripheral connections and the discoveries are endless. You can explore more about these possibilities. In this chapter, we discovered these possibilities by giving you some interesting starting points, by showing you how the BeagleBone Black can be used as a USB host in order to manage one or more devices, or as a USB device to emulate a USB peripheral. We also discovered how to manage a USB peripheral when a dedicated driver is not present, using a raw access to the bus.

In the next chapters, we'll present some kinds of peripherals that are not so common as serial ports and USB devices, as they are not directly accessible on a normal PC, only on an embedded device, such as the BeagleBone Black, which permits us to really discover and manage them. Let's see the I²C devices.

# 8

# Inter-integrated Circuit – I²C

In the previous chapter, we explored the serial ports and the USB bus (with the relative devices) that are peripherals typically used to connect a computer to another computer, or to a device, which is external to the main computer. Starting with this chapter, we are going to present some communication buses that are typically used to connect on-board devices, that is, the main computer with devices which are all placed on the same board.

One of the most important device classes is the Inter-integrated Circuit, which is abbreviated with the acronym I²C. Several devices use the I²C bus to communicate with the CPU, and in this chapter, we will give you a panoramic view of them: we'll see an **EEPROM** (a non-volatile memory), a **DAC (Digital to Analog Converter)**, and an **ADC (Analog to Digital Converter)**. For all of them, we'll see how these devices can be connected to the BeagleBone Black, and we can use the drivers to get access to their data.

## What is the I²C bus?

The **Inter-integrated Circuit** (**I²C**) is a multi-master, multi-slave, serial computer bus invented in order to simplify the board schematics, thanks to the fact that it needs two wires only (apart from the GND) to do its job. It's widely used in embedded computers to connect on-board sensors/actuators to the main CPU.

Despite the fact that the I²C bus is a multi-master, a typical configuration is a single master device (the CPU) connected to several slave devices (the sensors/actuators); for the USB bus, the master directs all the transfers. However, a main difference should be outlined: an I²C device can have a dedicated interrupt line connected to the CPU that can be used to signal that a message must be read by the master (in the USB bus, the interrupt messages go over the bus too!). So, a simple I²C connection needs two wires while they only, in case of interrupt lines, need three or more lines.

For more information on the working of the I²C bus, you can take a look at the URL http://en.wikipedia.org/wiki/I%C2%B2C.

# The electrical lines

The I²C bus lines are reported in the following table:

| Name | Description |
|------|-------------|
| **SCL (Serial Clock)** | This is the bus clock signal |
| **SDA (Serial Data)** | This is the bus data signal |
| GND | This is the common ground |

I haven't reported the interrupt line since, strictly speaking, it's not part of the I²C protocol. It is usually implemented as a dedicated interrupt line connected to a CPU's interrupt capable pin (GPIO lines).

The GND line has been added because it's needed for electrical reasons, as the I²C protocol just talks about the SCL and SDA signals only.

In case of multiple devices are connected, the I²C devices can be connected in parallel, as shown in the following diagram:

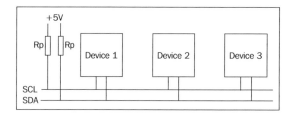

 The pull-up resistances **Rp** can be omitted in most cases, as most of the times an I²C controller integrates them by default.

# The I²C bus in Linux

Each I²C device has a well-defined 7 bit address that the master must use in order to communicate with a device. This address is not assigned at runtime and, as for the USB devices, it's assigned by the board designer by setting chip's pins.

Typically, the chip manufacturer sets the most significant 3 or 4 bits, and the board designer can set the remaining bits in order to suit his/her needs.

Another thing to be outlined regarding the I²C bus is that for each message, the master must specify whether the message wants to read or write data from the slave. This special action is done by adding a final bit (the least significant bit) to the slave address, and the master uses 0 to write data and 1 to read data from the slave.

As for the USB bus, we still have two main actors: master and slave. So, in the kernel, we will find both the device driver types.

Regarding the I²C master device, there is nothing special to do here since the proper driver is already up and running in the BeagleBone Black's default kernel configuration. However, in regards to the I²C devices to be connected to our BeagleBone Black, we can have several possibilities: external memories, I/O extenders, sensors, converters, and so on (the list can be very long).

Note that on some embedded systems, the on-chip I²C controller can be programmed to work as a master or as a slave device (this functionality must be supported by the respective driver). Strictly speaking, the developer can choose whether his/her I²C controller can be used to master the communication with other I²C devices or to act as an I²C device instead and then work as a simple slave. However, it's quite rare that an embedded system is used in the latter case; that's why in this book, we don't talk about this possibility.

The BeagleBone Black has three I²C buses (each managed by a dedicated I²C master), but one bus is not exported on the expansion connectors, one is already utilized to read EEPROMs on cape add-on boards (so, we can consider this as reserved; even if we can still use it, we must be aware of the fact to not interfere with the capes manager), and one bus is freely usable, as reported on the BeagleBone Black's support page at `http://beagleboard.org/support/bone101`. This is summarized in the following table:

| Name | SDA | SCL | Memory address |
|------|-----|-----|----------------|
| **I2c0** | Not exported | | 0x44E0B000 |
| **I2c1** | P9.18 or P9.26 | P9.17 or P9.24 | 0x4802A000 |
| **I2c2** | P9.20 or P9.22 | P9.19 or P9.21 | 0x4819C000 |

In the preceding table, the notation **P9.17** means that the pin **17** is on the expansion connector **P9**.

We can get these values directly from the BeagleBone Black firmware settings using the following command:

```
root@BeagleBone:~# dtc -I dtb -O dts <dtbo> | grep exclusive-use
```

Here, <dtbo> is one of the firmware files available in the /lib/firmware/ directory:

```
root@BeagleBone:~# ls /lib/firmware/BB-I2C*.dtbo

/lib/firmware/BB-I2C1-00A0.dtbo   /lib/firmware/BB-I2C1A1-00A0.dtbo
```

In the following example, we can figure out the involved pins using the following command:

```
root@BeagleBone:~# dtc -I dtb -O dts /lib/firmware/BB-I2C1-00A0.
dtbo | grep exclusive-use
        exclusive-use = "P9.18", "P9.17", "i2c1";
```

Note that under some Linux releases, these buses are named in the order in which they are enumerated, so their names may have nothing to do with the physical names. This is the reason, in the preceding table, I added the **Memory address** column, which reports the memory addresses where the I²C controllers are mapped to. Then, by checking the mapping in /sys/bus/i2c/devices, we can easily assign the right name to each bus. For example, on my board that runs Linux 3.8.x, the **i2c0** bus is mapped to the /dev/i2c-0 file but **i2c2** is mapped to the /dev/i2c-1 file, as shown in the following command:

```
root@BeagleBone:~# ls -l /sys/bus/i2c/devices/i2c-*

lrwxrwxrwx 1 root root 0 Apr 23 20:42 /sys/bus/i2c/devices/i2c-0 -> ../../../dev
ices/ocp.3/44e0b000.i2c/i2c-0

lrwxrwxrwx 1 root root 0 Apr 23 20:42 /sys/bus/i2c/devices/i2c-1 -> ../../../dev
ices/ocp.3/4819c000.i2c/i2c-1
```

So, on my system, I can see that the first device has a reasonable name, while the last device that Linux maps to the /dev/i2c-1 file is, in reality, the **i2c2** on the BeagleBone Black's reference manuals. Keep a watch on the I²C connections.

In our next example of managing a real device, using the raw access to the bus, we need to use the free bus, and we need to enable it. The magic to do this is using something similar to what we saw in the serial ports. We can use the following command:

```
root@BeagleBone:~# echo BB-I2C1 > /sys/devices/bone_capemgr.9/slots
```

> Note that the same results can be obtained using the config-pin command as follows:
>
> ```
> root@beaglebone:~# config-pin overlay BB-I2C1
> Loading BB-I2C1 overlay
> ```
>
> However, in this book, I'm going to use the echo method.

This should cause the following kernel messages activity:

```
bone-capemgr bone_capemgr.9: part_number 'BB-I2C1', version 'N/A'
bone-capemgr bone_capemgr.9: slot #7: generic override
bone-capemgr bone_capemgr.9: bone: Using override eeprom data at slot 7
bone-capemgr bone_capemgr.9: slot #7: 'Override Board Name,00A0,Override
Manuf,BB-I2C1'
bone-capemgr bone_capemgr.9: slot #7: Requesting part number/version based 'BB-
I2C1-00A0.dtb
bone-capemgr bone_capemgr.9: slot #7: Requesting firmware 'BB-I2C1-00A0.dtbo'
for board-name 'Override Board Name', version '00A0'
bone-capemgr bone_capemgr.9: slot #7: dtbo 'BB-I2C1-00A0.dtbo' loaded;
converting to live tree
bone-capemgr bone_capemgr.9: slot #7: #2 overlays
omap_i2c 4802a000.i2c: bus 2 rev0.11 at 100 kHz
omap_i2c 4802a000.i2c: unable to select pin group
bone-capemgr bone_capemgr.9: slot #7: Applied #2 overlays.
```

At this point, the new bus should be present:

```
root@BeagleBone:~# ls -l /sys/bus/i2c/devices/i2c-*
lrwxrwxrwx 1 root root 0 Apr 23 20:42 /sys/bus/i2c/devices/i2c-0 -> ../../../dev
ices/ocp.3/44e0b000.i2c/i2c-0
lrwxrwxrwx 1 root root 0 Apr 23 20:42 /sys/bus/i2c/devices/i2c-1 -> ../../../dev
ices/ocp.3/4819c000.i2c/i2c-1
lrwxrwxrwx 1 root root 0 Apr 24 13:16 /sys/bus/i2c/devices/i2c-2 -> ../../../dev
ices/ocp.3/4802a000.i2c/i2c-2
```

# Getting access to I²C devices

Now we are ready to manage the real I²C devices. We can find tons of supported devices in the Linux kernel tree, which are usually grouped according to their specific operations; so, for instance, all the I²C real-time clock chips are under the `drivers/rtc/` directory, while the I²C EEPROMs are under the `drivers/misc/eeprom/` directory, and so on.

For example, we're going to use the following development board that carries five I²C devices:

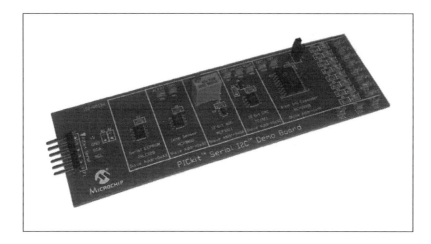

 The device can be purchased at (or by surfing the Internet)

`http://www.cosino.io/product/i2c-sensors-board`.

On this board, we have an EEPROM, an ADC, a DAC, a temperature sensor, and an I/O expander, so it's perfect to show you how the I²C bus works, and how the preceding device classes can be accessed within our BeagleBone Black.

First of all, we must complete the electrical connections; so, in the following table, I reported the connection between the BeagleBone Black's pins and the I²C developing board's pins:

| BeagleBone Black pins – label | I²C development board pins – label |
|---|---|
| P9.4 – **VCC** | 2 – **VCC** |
| P9.17 – **SCL** | 5 – **SCL** |
| P9.18 – **SDA** | 4 – **SDA** |
| P9.2 – **GND** | 3 – **GND** |

Now, if everything has been well connected, by running the following command, we should get a list of the addresses of the available I²C devices:

```
root@BeagleBone:~# i2cdetect -y -r 2
     0  1  2  3  4  5  6  7  8  9  a  b  c  d  e  f
00:          -- -- -- -- -- -- -- -- -- -- -- -- --
10: -- -- -- -- -- -- -- -- -- -- -- -- -- -- -- --
20: 20 -- -- -- -- -- -- -- -- -- -- -- -- -- -- --
30: -- -- -- -- -- -- -- -- -- -- -- -- -- -- -- --
40: -- -- -- -- -- -- -- -- 48 49 -- -- -- 4d -- --
50: 50 51 52 53 54 55 56 57 -- -- -- -- -- -- -- --
60: -- -- -- -- -- -- -- -- -- -- -- -- -- -- -- --
70: -- -- -- -- -- -- -- --
```

If we take a closer look at the I²C board, we can see that each device has reported its I²C address:

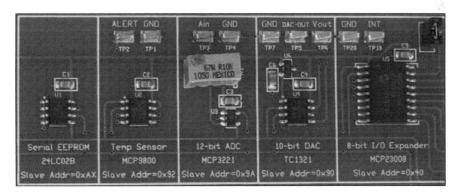

 Note that the EEPROM has up to eight valid I²C addresses.

The following table reports the correspondences between 7 bit and 8 bit notations:

| Device | I²C address as reported on the board | I²C address as reported by Linux |
|---|---|---|
| EEPROM | 0xAx | 0x5x |
| Temperature sensor | 0x92 | 0x49 |
| 12-bit ADC | 0x9A | 0x4d |
| 10-bit DAC | 0x90 | 0x48 |
| 8-bit I/O expander | 0x40 | 0x20 |

> The 8-bit address is just the corresponding 7-bit plus one 0-bit as LSB.

So, we can easily verify that all the devices are now available. However, we have not finished yet; in fact, even if all the devices are detected, they are still not available as device files in the BeagleBone Black's /dev directory because the system has not loaded the proper device drivers yet. To do so, we must first load a proper driver, and then write a suitable configuration file for the kernel in order to enable it.

Let's see how to do this by using some examples. We'll show you how to get access to the EEPROM, ADC, and DAC.

> Even if the other two I²C devices are supported by the Linux kernel, they have some issues on the BeagleBone Black's kernel 3.8.x. This is the first reason I didn't expose them.
>
> The second is due to a page limit for this book.

# The EEPROM

The EEPROM is based on the chip family named AT24, and the corresponding driver is already statically compiled in the kernel because the BeagleBone Black cape's management system uses an EEPROM based on that chip.

We can verify this by listing the currently enabled AT24 devices on our BeagleBone Black with the following command:

```
root@BeagleBone:~# ls /sys/bus/i2c/drivers/at24/
0-0050 1-0054 1-0055 1-0056 1-0057 bind  uevent  unbind
```

On the bus i2c-0, at address 0x50, there is a device, so let's inspect it:

```
root@BeagleBone:~# ls /sys/bus/i2c/drivers/at24/0-0050
driver eeprom modalias name       power subsystem uevent
root@BeagleBone:~# cat /sys/bus/i2c/drivers/at24/0-0050/name
24c256
```

Yes! It's an EEPROM device based on the AT24 family. So, now that the driver is already up and running, we only need the configuration file the reader can find into the `chapter_08/BB-EEPROM-A24-00A0.dts` file in the book's example code repository. In the following snippet, are reported the main configuration settings:

```
/* Set the desired clock frequency */
clock-frequency = <100000>;

/* Define the EEPROM device as based on at24c256
 * and with I2C address 0x50
 */
eeprom: eeprom@50 {
        compatible = "at24,24c02";
        reg        = <0x50>;
};
```

This special syntax is suitable for the **Device Tree Compiler** (the `dtc` command) and defines our I²C device according to the hardware settings.

> The **Device Tree Compiler** is used to convert the human-editable device tree source format (the `.dts` file) to the compact device tree blob representation (the `.dtb` file) used by the kernel.
>
> The code in the preceding example just defines the bus clock frequency, the EEPROM type, and its I²C address. For more information on these files and their syntaxes, you may take a look at the URL `http://devicetree.org/Device_Tree_Usage`.

Now we should compile it using the following command:

```
root@BeagleBone:~# dtc -O dtb -o /lib/firmware/BB-EEPROM-A24-00A0.dtbo
-b 0 -@ BB-EEPROM-A24-00A0.dts
```

After this, we can enable our new EEPROM using a command similar to the command used earlier to set up a new kernel configuration:

```
root@BeagleBone:~# echo BB-EEPROM-A24 > /sys/devices/bone_capemgr.9/slots
```

Now, if we take a look at the BeagleBone Black's kernel messages, we should see the following activity:

```
bone-capemgr bone_capemgr.9: part_number 'BB-EEPROM-A24', version 'N/A'
bone-capemgr bone_capemgr.9: slot #8: generic override
```

```
bone-capemgr bone_capemgr.9: bone: Using override eeprom data at slot 8
bone-capemgr bone_capemgr.9: slot #8: 'Override Board Name,00A0,Override
Manuf,BB-EEPROM-A24'
bone-capemgr bone_capemgr.9: slot #8: Requesting part number/version
based 'BB-EEPROM-A24-00A0.dtbo
bone-capemgr bone_capemgr.9: slot #8: Requesting firmware 'BB-EEPROM-A24-
00A0.dtbo' for board-name 'Override Board Name', version '00A0'
bone-capemgr bone_capemgr.9: slot #8: dtbo 'BB-EEPROM-A24-00A0.dtbo'
loaded; converting to live tree
bone-capemgr bone_capemgr.9: slot #8: #1 overlays
at24 2-0050: 256 byte 24c02 EEPROM, writable, 1 bytes/write
bone-capemgr bone_capemgr.9: slot #8: Applied #1 overlays.
```

Now our new EEPROM should be enabled:

```
root@BeagleBone:~# ls /sys/bus/i2c/drivers/at24/
0-0050  1-0054  1-0055  1-0056  1-0057  2-0050  bind  uevent  unbind
```

The new directory is 2-0050, which represents our EEPROM, so now, we can use
the eeprom file to read/write our desired data. For instance, we can write a string,
and then we can reread it using the following commands:

```
root@BeagleBone:~# echo "Testing message" > /sys/bus/i2c/drivers/at24/2-
0050/eeprom
root@BeagleBone:~# strings /sys/bus/i2c/drivers/at24/2-0050/eeprom
Testing message
```

> The strings command has been used in order to discard all
> non ASCII characters because the cat command will read all
> the EEPROM content, not only the string we wrote.

# The ADC chip

The ADC chip is based on the MCP3221 that is managed by the mcp3021.c driver,
which, most probably, is not included in the default kernel distribution that runs on
your BeagleBone Black. You can verify this situation by taking a look at the following
directory for the mcp3021.ko filename, as reported in the following command line:

```
root@BeagleBone:~# ls /lib/modules/$(uname -r)/kernel/drivers/hwmon/
mcp3021.ko
ls: cannot access /lib/modules/3.8.13-bone47/kernel/drivers/hwmon/
mcp3021.ko: No such file or directory
```

In this case, we have to compile the driver, as described in *The Linux kernel* section of *Chapter 3, Compiling versus Cross-compiling*, and then copy it to the BeagleBone Black's distribution using the following command in the host PC:

```
$ scp KERNEL/drivers/hwmon/mcp3021.ko root@192.168.7.2:
```

> This is the current directory where the build_kernel.sh command has been executed.
>
> Also, note that in *The Linux kernel* section of *Chapter 3, Compiling versus Cross-compiling*, we recompiled the kernel release 3.13.x. If you are running a different release, you must compile the corresponding kernel, or the resulting module will not load it at all.
>
> For example, if the current kernel is 3.8.x (as in my case), I will use the following command to get the right sources:
>
> ```
> $ git checkout am33x-v3.8
> ```
>
> Then, I will rerun build_kernel.sh as done earlier.

To enable the driver compilation, we must go to the kernel configuration menu, and enable the setting by navigating to **Device Drivers | Hardware Monitoring support | Microchip MCP3021 and compatibles** before executing the building command (see the *Compiling the kernel* section in *Chapter 3, Compiling versus Cross-compiling*).

After the driver compilation, we have to install it on the BeagleBone Black. To do so, we simply have to copy the mcp3021.ko file to the proper directory, as reported in the following command line:

```
root@BeagleBone:~# mv mcp3021.ko /lib/modules/$(uname -r)/kernel/drivers/hwmon/
```

Then, we have to run the depmod command in order to rebuild the module dependencies:

```
root@BeagleBone:~# depmod -a
```

Now we need only the proper kernel configuration. As before, we can use the dtc utility on the chapter_08/BB-ADC-MCP322-00A0.dts file in the book's example code repository. The file is very similar to the EEPROM's one presented earlier and it's self-explanatory. However, let me discuss the following snippet in order to outline the important lines:

```
/* Set the desired clock frequency */
clock-frequency = <100000>;
```

```
/* Define the ADC device as based on mcp3221
 * and with I2C address 0x4d
 */
adc: adc@4d {
        compatible = "mcp3221";
        reg        = <0x4d>;
};
```

Well, let's compile it, as done earlier:

```
root@BeagleBone:~# dtc -O dtb -o /lib/firmware/BB-ADC-MCP322-00A0.dtbo
-b 0 -@ BB-ADC-MCP322-00A0.dts
```

Then, we enable the ADC using the following command:

```
root@BeagleBone:~# echo BB-ADC-MCP322 > /sys/devices/bone_capemgr.9/slots
```

The kernel activity in this case is reported as follows:

```
bone-capemgr bone_capemgr.9: part_number 'BB-ADC-MCP322', version 'N/A'

bone-capemgr bone_capemgr.9: slot #8: generic override

bone-capemgr bone_capemgr.9: bone: Using override eeprom data at slot 8

bone-capemgr bone_capemgr.9: slot #8: 'Override Board Name,00A0,Override
Manuf,BB-ADC-MCP322'

bone-capemgr bone_capemgr.9: slot #8: Requesting part number/version
based 'BB-ADC-MCP322-00A0.dtbo

bone-capemgr bone_capemgr.9: slot #8: Requesting firmware 'BB-ADC-MCP322-
00A0.dtbo' for board-name 'Override Board Name', version '00A0'

bone-capemgr bone_capemgr.9: slot #8: dtbo 'BB-ADC-MCP322-00A0.dtbo'
loaded; converting to live tree

bone-capemgr bone_capemgr.9: slot #8: #1 overlays

bone-capemgr bone_capemgr.9: slot #8: Applied #1 overlays.
```

If everything works well, the ADC data can now be accessed using the following command:

```
root@BeagleBone:~# cat /sys/bus/i2c/drivers/mcp3021/2-004d/in0_input
1526
```

The preceding data is just a random value as the input pin is floating; if we wish to get well-defined data, we can try to connect the **Ain** pin to GND, and then to VCC; we should then get an output as follows:

```
root@BeagleBone:~# cat /sys/bus/i2c/drivers/mcp3021/2-004d/in0_input
0
root@BeagleBone:~# cat /sys/bus/i2c/drivers/mcp3021/2-004d/in0_input
4095
```

We get exactly the expected values as the GND corresponds to 0, and VCC is the maximum allowed value, corresponding **4095** ($2^{12}$-1).

> To convert the raw data value and the input voltage present in the **Ain** pin, you can use the following formula:
>
> Vout = Vcc * (raw_value / 4095)
>
> Here, *Vcc* is the maximum value in volts that the system can read, *raw_value* is the current read value, and *Vout* is the converted voltage value.

# Accessing the bus directly

Now, as for a USB bus, we should take a look at how we can get direct access to the I²C bus. In the same manner, as for USB devices, if one of them doesn't have a dedicated driver, they can be managed directly from the user space. The only problem that may arise is if the I²C device generates interrupts; in this case, we cannot manage these signals from the user-space and a kernel driver must be used. However, this is a rare case and the presented technique can be used in most cases.

For example, we're going to manage the DAC chip named **TC1321**. If we take a look at the chip's datasheet, we can see that its functioning is very simple: it has one 16-bit register at offset `0x00`, where we can write the digital data to be converted.

> The datasheet is available at the URL `http://ww1.microchip.com/downloads/en/DeviceDoc/21387C.pdf`.

The register has the following format:

| Data register = first byte | | | | | | | | Data register = second byte | | | | | | | |
|---|---|---|---|---|---|---|---|---|---|---|---|---|---|---|---|
| D9 | D8 | D7 | D6 | D5 | D4 | D3 | D2 | D1 | D0 | - | - | - | - | - | - |
| MSB | X | X | X | X | X | X | X | X | LSB | - | - | - | - | - | - |

So, for example, if we wish to write the hexadecimal value 0x41 in the DAC, we must build the 16-bit hexadecimal value 0x0140 (that is, 0x41 is shifted six positions to the left).

Remember what we did at the beginning of this chapter. We have to create the I²C bus device, and we should use this bus device in order to get access to the bus. We can do it using the following command:

```
root@BeagleBone:~# echo BB-I2C1 > /sys/devices/bone_capemgr.9/slots
```

Now the /dev/i2c-2 device is ready, and we can run the program in the chapter_08/i2c_dac/i2c_dac.c file in the book's example code repository to manage this chip. The two reg2value() and value2reg() functions are used to convert the data exchanged with the chip, while the main() function is the core part of the program.

After opening the /dev/i2c-2 device, which corresponds to our I²C bus, we set the I²C address of the device we wish to talk to using the ioctl() system call as follows:

```
/* Select the I2C bus to talk with */
ret = ioctl(fd, I2C_SLAVE, I2C_SLAVE_ADDR);
if (ret < 0) {
    fprintf(stderr, "%s: cannot acquire access to address 0x%x\n",
            NAME, I2C_SLAVE_ADDR);
    exit(1);
}
```

Now, the code has two different behaviors according to the command line used. If the user uses the following command line, we get the following result:

```
root@BeagleBone:~# ./i2c_dac 100
```

The program will write the value `100` to the DAC's register using the following code:

```
/* Convert the user's value into a suitable form for the DAC */
value2reg(val, &wbuf[1], &wbuf[2]);

/* Write the data to the device */
ret = write(fd, wbuf, sizeof(wbuf));
if (ret != sizeof(wbuf)) {
        fprintf(stderr, "%s: failed to write: %m\n", NAME);
        exit(1);
}
```

On the other hand, if we run the following command line, we get the following result:

```
root@BeagleBone:~/i2c# ./i2c_dac
100
```

The program will read the DAC's register using the following code:

```
ret = read(fd, rbuf, sizeof(rbuf));
if (ret != sizeof(rbuf)) {
        fprintf(stderr, "%s: failed to read: %m\n", NAME);
        exit(1);
}

/* Convert the just read data to a readable form */
reg2value(rbuf[0], rbuf[1], &val);
```

Now, to do a simple check in order to verify that the preceding code is really working, we can shortcut the pin labeled **Ain** of the ADC to the pin labeled **Vout** of the DAC (see the image of the preceding I²C board). In this situation, we can write an analog voltage on the DAC, and then read it using the ADC:

```
root@BeagleBone:~/i2c# ./i2c_dac 100
root@BeagleBone:~/i2c# cat /sys/bus/i2c/drivers/mcp3021/2-004d/in0_input
296
root@BeagleBone:~/i2c# ./i2c_dac 500
root@BeagleBone:~/i2c# cat /sys/bus/i2c/drivers/mcp3021/2-004d/in0_input
1472
```

Note that the digital values that are read from the ADC and are written to the DAC do not perfectly correspond due to electrical reasons, and also because they have different resolutions. However, we can notice that, more or less, `1472` is five times `296`, as `500` is with respect to the value `100`.

> Note that in order to access the registers of an I²C device, the user may also use the utilities in the `i2c-tools` package:
>
> ```
> root@beaglebone:~# apt-cache show i2c-tools
> Package: i2c-tools
> Version: 3.1.0-2
> Installed-Size: 209
> Maintainer: Aurelien Jarno <aurel32@debian.org>
> Architecture: armhf
> Depends: libc6 (>= 2.13-28), perl, adduser, udev | makedev
> Suggests: libi2c-dev, python-smbus
> Conflicts: lm-sensors (<< 1:3.0.0-1)
> Description-en: heterogeneous set of I2C tools for Linux
>  This package contains a heterogeneous set of I2C tools for
> Linux: a bus probing tool, a chip dumper, register-level
> access helpers, EEPROM  decoding scripts, and more.
> Homepage: http://www.lm-sensors.org
>  ...
> ```
>
> However, in some circumstances, these tools cannot be used efficiently, so it's important to know how to write the custom code.

# Summary

In this chapter, we learned about the I²C bus, and how we can use the Linux device drivers to access the I²C device. We also explored how we can write our own I²C driver as a user-space application.

However, even if the I²C bus is widely used in every embedded computer, and a large variety of I²C peripherals exist, another on-board bus can be found on most systems, that is, the SPI bus and its devices. So, now, it's time to go to the next chapter.

# 9

# Serial Peripheral Interface – SPI

As we have already seen in the previous chapter, the I²C's similar features exist, and one of them is the **Serial Peripheral Interface** (**SPI**). However, as opposed to the I²C bus, this bus can transfer data at higher rates than I²C, and since it is full-duplex, the data transfer can take place bidirectionally. Due to these features, the SPI bus is normally used to implement an efficient data stream for multimedia applications (LCDs/video), digital signal processing and/or telecommunications devices (Ethernet, CAN, serial ports, and so on), and SD cards. However, despite this fact, it can be used to communicate with standard sensors, ADC/DAC converters, and other similar devices too.

In order to demonstrate the versatility of the SPI bus, in this chapter, we're going to present a simple temperature sensor management using a thermocouple sensor and a more complex device, such as a mini LCD display.

## What is the SPI bus?

The SPI bus is a full-duplex, single master, multi-slave, synchronous serial interface; as for the I²C bus, it is used for the on-board connection of sensor chips with the main CPU. This bus requires at least (apart from the GND signal) three wires plus one chip select signal per slave. This line is typically called **Slave Select** (**SS**) or **Chip Select** (**CS**), and usually, it's active low (that is, the master must set it to 0 to enable the desired slave chip).

A **full-duplex** is a connection that can transmit and receive at the same time on the bus.

**Synchronous** means that the clock is sent along with the data (in this case, it is the master that provides the clock).

**Single master** and **multi-slave** mean that in the bus there is only one master, who directs the communication, while more than one slave can be connected to the bus.

**Serial data** is transmitted one bit at a time over the bus.

The communication starts when the bus master configures the clock, using a frequency supported by the connected slave devices, and then the master selects a slave using the proper select line. For each SPI clock cycle, the master sends a bit on the **MOSI** line (the acronym is **Master Output Slave Input** and represents the output line of the master), which is read by the slave, while the slave sends a bit on the **MISO** line (meaning **Master Input Slave Output** and representing the input line of the master), and the master reads it. Note that this sequence is maintained in case of one-directional data transfer only. The most important thing is that each slave on the bus that is not activated for the data transmission must drop both the input clock and MOSI signals, and must not drive MISO in order to eliminate interference with the selected slave output. It's quite obvious that in an SPI communication, the master must select one slave at a time only.

Here is quite clear that respecting to I²C, whereas the bus is request/reply sharing a single line apart the clock, the SPI bus has two communications happening in parallel: the slave writes while the master is writing at the same time. This is why we have separated the MOSI/MISO lines.

Typically, SPI communications are 8-bit wide even if other sizes are also common: 16-bit words for touchscreen controllers or audio codecs, or 12-bit words for many digital-to-analog or analog-to-digital converters. The intricate details of how the SPI bus works is out of the scope of this book. You can find more information on this at http://en.wikipedia. org/wiki/Serial_Peripheral_Interface_Bus.

# The electrical lines

The SPI bus lines are reported in the following table:

| Name | Description |
| --- | --- |
| SCLK: Serial clock | This is the bus clock signal |
| MOSI: Master Out Slave In | This is the bus data signal (Master Output Slave Input) |

| Name | Description |
|---|---|
| MISO: Master In Slave Out | This is the bus data signal (Master Input Slave Output) |
| SS: Slave Select | This is the chip or slave select signal (one per slave) |
| GND | This is the common ground |

It's quite common that an SPI controller has a few SS lines (usually 2 or 3), so when more SPI devices are needed at once, a trick must be used. The solution is to generate the needed SS signals using the common GPIO lines managed by the driver, instead of by the controller hardware itself.

Despite the fact that this behavior can permit a very large number of devices to be connected to a single master, it slows down the whole bus performances, as the signals are driven in the software rather than in the hardware. Also, note that this feature must be supported by the SPI master controller's device driver.

In the case of there being multiple devices connected, they must be connected in parallel. However, the SS signals must be routed to one slave at a time:

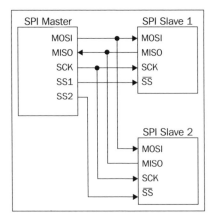

# The SPI bus in Linux

The BeagleBone Black has two SPI buses, as reported in the BeagleBone Black's support page at http://beagleboard.org/support/bone101, and is summarized in the following table:

| Name | MISO | MOSI | SCLK | SS0 | SS1 |
|---|---|---|---|---|---|
| spi1 | P9.21 | P9.18 | P9.22 | P9.17 | Not available |
| spi2 | P9.29 | P9.30 | P9.31 | P9.20 or P9.28 | P9.19 or P9.42 |

In the preceding table, the notation **P9_18** means that the pin **18** is on the expansion connector **P9**.

These values can be directly fetched from the BeagleBone Black's firmware settings using the following command:

```
root@BeagleBone:~# dtc -I dtb -O dts <dtbo> | grep
exclusive-use
```

Here, `<dtbo>` is one of the firmware files available in the `/lib/firmware/` directory:

```
root@BeagleBone:~# ls /lib/firmware/BB-SPIDEV*.dtbo
/lib/firmware/BB-SPIDEV0-00A0.dtbo   /lib/firmware/BB-
SPIDEV1A1-00A0.dtbo
/lib/firmware/BB-SPIDEV1-00A0.dtbo
```

In the following example, we can figure out the involved pins using the following command:

```
root@BeagleBone:~# dtc -I dtb -O dts /lib/firmware/BB-
SPIDEV0-00A0.dtbo | grep exclusive-use
        exclusive-use = "P9.17", "P9.18", "P9.21",
"P9.22", "spi0";
```

The BeagleBone Black's default configuration reserves the `spi1` bus to the HDMI support. In fact, if we try to enable it with the following command, we get the following error message:

```
root@BeagleBone:~# echo BB-SPIDEV1 > /sys/devices/bone_capemgr.9/slots
-bash: echo: write error: File exists
```

Then, in the kernel messages, we can read these reasons:

```
bone-capemgr bone_capemgr.9: part_number 'BB-SPIDEV1', version 'N/A'
bone-capemgr bone_capemgr.9: slot #7: generic override
bone-capemgr bone_capemgr.9: bone: Using override eeprom data at slot 7
bone-capemgr bone_capemgr.9: slot #7: 'Override Board Name,00A0,Override
Manuf,BB-SPIDEV1'
bone-capemgr bone_capemgr.9: slot #7: Requesting part number/version
based 'BB-SPIDEV1-00A0.dtbo
bone-capemgr bone_capemgr.9: slot #7: Requesting firmware 'BB-SPIDEV1-
00A0.dtbo' for board-name 'Override Board Name', version '00A0'
bone-capemgr bone_capemgr.9: slot #7: dtbo 'BB-SPIDEV1-00A0.dtbo' loaded;
converting to live tree
bone-capemgr bone_capemgr.9: slot #7: BB-SPIDEV1 conflict P9.31 (#5:BB-
BONELT-HDMI)
bone-capemgr bone_capemgr.9: slot #7: Failed verification
```

One possible solution to this situation can be to disable the HDMI support (we're going to use this solution in the next section), but, of course, the simplest one is to use the other bus. So, let's enable this with the following command:

```
root@BeagleBone:~# echo BB-SPIDEV0 > /sys/devices/bone_capemgr.9/slots
```

This should cause the following kernel message activity:

```
bone-capemgr bone_capemgr.9: part_number 'BB-SPIDEV0', version 'N/A'
bone-capemgr bone_capemgr.9: slot #7: generic override
bone-capemgr bone_capemgr.9: bone: Using override eeprom data at slot 7
bone-capemgr bone_capemgr.9: slot #7: 'Override Board Name,00A0,Override
Manuf,BB-SPIDEV0'
bone-capemgr bone_capemgr.9: slot #7: Requesting part number/version
based 'BB-SPIDEV0-00A0.dtbo
bone-capemgr bone_capemgr.9: slot #7: Requesting firmware 'BB-SPIDEV0-
00A0.dtbo' for board-name 'Override Board Name', version '00A0'
bone-capemgr bone_capemgr.9: slot #7: dtbo 'BB-SPIDEV0-00A0.dtbo' loaded;
converting to live tree
bone-capemgr bone_capemgr.9: slot #7: #2 overlays
edma-dma-engine edma-dma-engine.0: allocated channel for 0:19
edma-dma-engine edma-dma-engine.0: allocated channel for 0:18
edma-dma-engine edma-dma-engine.0: allocated channel for 0:17
edma-dma-engine edma-dma-engine.0: allocated channel for 0:16
bone-capemgr bone_capemgr.9: slot #7: Applied #2 overlays.
```

No errors are reported and the SPI devices are now available:

```
root@BeagleBone:~# ls -l /sys/bus/spi/devices/
total 0
lrwxrwxrwx 1 root root 0 Apr 23 21:09 spi1.0 -> ../../../devices/
ocp.3/48030000.spi/spi_master/spi1/spi1.0
lrwxrwxrwx 1 root root 0 Apr 23 21:09 spi1.1 -> ../../../devices/
ocp.3/48030000.spi/spi_master/spi1/spi1.1
```

 Note that the `/dev/spi1.0` SPI device is not referred to for the whole bus, as for the I²C bus, but it points to the SPI device connected to the first chip select line. Meanwhile, the `/dev/spi1.1` device points to the SPI device connected to the second chip select line.

This setting allows the user to have raw access to the bus that is quite generic. This will be used in the following section, where we'll describe how to manage a simple SPI device using this raw access mode.

# Getting access to the SPI devices

As already stated in the previous section, there exist several SPI slaves, and since we have to choose one of them to present here, I decided to show you how to manage an LCD display.

I'm going to use the following tiny LCD display, which can be used in simple applications, because it's cheap and well supported by the BeagleBone Black's kernel:

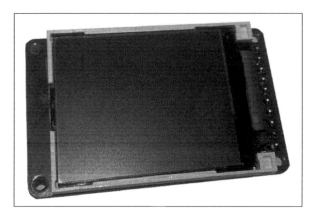

 The device can be purchased at (or by surfing the Internet) `http://www.cosino.io/product/color-tft-lcd-1-8-160x128`.

First of all, we must do the electrical connections, so in the following table, I have reported the correspondence between the BeagleBone Black's pins and the LCD pins:

| BeagleBone Black pins – label | LCD pins – label |
| --- | --- |
| P9.4 – VCC | 9 – VCC |
| P9.29 – MISO | Not connected |
| P9.30 – MOSI | 4 – MOSI |
| P9.31 – SCLK | 3 – SCK |
| P9.28 – SS0 | 5 – TFT_CS |
| P9.25 | 7 – D/C |
| P9.27 | 8 – RESET |
| P8.19 | 1 – LITE |
| P9.2 – GND | 10 – GND |

You can note that we used the SPI dedicated pins, plus some GPIOs lines. This configuration is quite typical in the SPI connections since it's more efficient to use additional lines to specify the special data, which means using proper SPI messages to manage the device. In our LCD, we will use the D/C line (the name **D/C** is for **Data/Command**) to specify which data is simple graphical data and which data contains special commands for the LCD instead. The meaning of the **RESET** line is obvious, while the LITE line is used to manage the backlight intensity (note that this line is not a simple GPIO but it's a PWM line).

The PWM lines are special lines that can generate a *pulse width* signal. For space reasons, I cannot explain them in this book, but from this example, you can start to learn about a possible usage of these signals and then read more about them on the Internet.

Now, we should verify that the correct driver is available in our system; we can do this using the following command:

```
root@BeagleBone:~# zcat /proc/config.gz | grep -i st7735
CONFIG_FB_ST7735=y
```

In the kernel configuration, the driver is statically linked to the kernel, but it's ok to have it as a module; in this case, the output should look something like this:

```
CONFIG_FB_ST7735=m
```

Note that if we do get any output, then we must enable the driver in the kernel configuration menu by navigating to **Device Drivers | Graphics support | Support for frame buffer devices | ST7735 framebuffer support**, and then recompile the kernel (see the *Compiling the kernel* section of *Chapter 3, Compiling versus Cross-compiling*, or the *Writing our own device driver* section of *Chapter 5, Device Drivers*).

After checking the driver, we also need a proper DTS file to set up the kernel. Writing it from scratch is quite difficult, so it is better to download it from the Internet from one of the several BeagleBone Black's dedicated sites.

I got a valid DTS file from the following URL using the wget command:

```
root@BeagleBone:~# wget https://raw.githubusercontent.com/beagleboard/
devicetree-source/master/arch/arm/boot/dts/cape-bone-adafruit-lcd-00A0.
dts
```

This file is quite complex, but it's well commented out, so let's see it in detail.

 You can read more about the device tree and its syntax at the URL `http://devicetree.org/Device_Tree_Usage`.

You can also find this file in `chapter_09/cape-bone-adafruit-lcd-00A0.dts` in the book's example code repository.

The first section describes the pins used:

```
/* state the resources this cape uses */
exclusive-use =
        /* the pin header uses */
        "P8.19",          /* bl: ehrpwm2A */
        "P9.27",          /* lcd: gpio3_19 */
        "P9.25",          /* lcd: gpio3_21 */
        "P9.31",          /* spi: spi1_sclk */
        "P9.29",          /* spi: spi1_d0 */
        "P9.30",          /* spi: spi1_d1 */
        "P9.28",          /* spi: spi1_cs0 */
        /* the hardware IP uses */
        "gpio3_19",
        "gpio3_21",
        "ehrpwm2A",
        "spi1";
```

Here are the pins needed to manage the LCD. However, this is a descriptive section only, and the effective settings are located in the section labeled `fragment@0`:

```
fragment@0 {
        target = <&am33xx_pinmux>;
        __overlay__ {
                pwm_backlight_pins: pinmux_pwm_backlight_pins {
                        pinctrl-single,pins = <
                                0x020   0x4         /* gpmc_ad8.gpio0_22 | MODE4 */
                        >;
                };

                bone_adafruit_lcd_pins: pinmux_bone_adafruit_lcd_pins {
                        pinctrl-single,pins = <
                                0x1a4 0x17          /* mcasp0_fsr.gpio3_19 */
                                0x1ac 0x17          /* mcasp0_ahclkx.gpio3_21 */
                        >;
                };

                bone_adafruit_spi1_pins: pinmux_adafruit_spi1_pins {
                        pinctrl-single,pins = <
```

```
                          0x190 0x33       /* mcasp0_aclkx.spi1_sclk */
                          0x194 0x33       /* mcasp0_fsx.spi1_d0 */
                          0x198 0x13       /* mcasp0_axr0.spi1_d1 */
                          0x19c 0x13       /* mcasp0_ahclkr.spi1_cs0 */
                  >;
          };
      };
  };
```

All the pins have a proper description, but the magic numbers used to set them up are quite obscure. However, BeagleBone Black is really well supported on the Internet, and you can take a look at these two documents regarding the GPIO settings in order to discover what the numbers refer to at https://github.com/derekmolloy/boneDeviceTree/tree/master/docs.

This section declares all the needed pins, dividing them into three main groups:

- The PWM pin for the backlight
- The LCD control pins (**D/C** and **RESET**)
- The SPI controller's pins

Note that the DTS file uses the spi1 bus, so we have to disable the HDMI interface in order to use it for our LCD (we will describe this action very soon).

The next sections labeled fragment@1 and fragment@2 are used to enable the BeagleBone Black's PWM subsystem. While in fragment@3, we found the LCD settings, which is the part that is really interesting to us:

```
          fragment@3 {
          target = <&spi1>;

          __overlay__ {
                  #address-cells = <1>;
                  #size-cells = <0>;

                  status        = "okay";
                  pinctrl-names = "default";
                  pinctrl-0     = <&bone_adafruit_spi1_pins>;

                  lcd@0 {
                          #address-cells = <1>;
                          #size-cells = <0>;

                          compatible = "adafruit,tft-lcd-1.8-red",
  "sitronix,st7735";
```

```
                                reg = <0>;

                                spi-max-frequency = <8000000>;
                                spi-cpol;
                                spi-cpha;

                                pinctrl-names = "default";
                                pinctrl-0 = <&bone_adafruit_lcd_pins>;

                                st7735-rst = <&gpio4 19 0>;
                                st7735-dc = <&gpio4 21 0>;
                        };
                };
        };
```

The target of the section is the spi1 bus, and the next settings used are to enable
the pins' group, named bone_adafruit_spi1_pins. The LCD's driver settings are
located in the subsection labeled lcd@0. In particular, the file sets some SPI settings
(spi-max-frequency, spi-cpol, and spi-cpha). It declares that we use the LCD
control pins group named bone_adafruit_lcd_pins, and it tells the driver which
pin must be used as a **RESET** signal and **D/C** signal.

The last section describes the PWM settings:

```
    fragment@4 {
            target = <&ocp>;

            /* avoid stupid warning */
            #address-cells = <1>;
            #size-cells = <1>;

            __overlay__ {
                    adafruit-tft-backlight {
                            compatible      = "pwm-backlight";
                            pinctrl-names   = "default";
                            pinctrl-0       = <&pwm_backlight_pins>;

                            pwms = <&ehrpwm2 0 500000 0>;

                            pwm-names = "st7735fb";
```

```
                    brightness-levels = <0 1 2 3 4 5 6 7 8 9 10 11
   12 13 14 15 16 17 18 19 20 21 22 23 24 25 26 27 28 29 30 31 32 33 34
   35 36 37 38 39 40 41 42 43 44 45 46 47 48 49 50 51 52 53 54 55 56 57
   58 59 60 61 62 63 64 65 66 67 68 69 70 71 72 73 74 75 76 77 78 79 80
   81 82 83 84 85 86 87 88 89 90 91 92 93 94 95 96 97 98 99 100>;
                    default-brightness-level = <101>;
            };
        };
    };
```

In the LCD section, the file defines the backlight pin group named pwm_backlight
_pins, and tells the driver which is the pin and where to send the PWM output.
It then lists the allowed backlight brightness levels that the user can set from the
user space.

Well, now we're ready, and we only need to compile the preceding DTS file using
the following command:

```
root@BeagleBone:~# dtc -O dtb -o /lib/firmware/cape-bone-lcd-00A0.dtbo -b
0 -@ cape-bone-adafruit-lcd-00A0.dts
```

We can enable the LCD using the usual echo command:

```
root@BeagleBone:~# echo cape-bone-lcd > /sys/devices/bone_capemgr.9/slots
-bash: echo: write error: File exists
```

Ouch, we got an error! Let's see what happens in the kernel messages:

```
bone-capemgr bone_capemgr.9: part_number 'cape-bone-lcd', version 'N/A'

bone-capemgr bone_capemgr.9: slot #7: generic override

bone-capemgr bone_capemgr.9: bone: Using override eeprom data at slot 7

bone-capemgr bone_capemgr.9: slot #7: 'Override Board Name,00A0,Override
Manuf,cape-bone-lcd'

bone-capemgr bone_capemgr.9: slot #7: Requesting part number/version
based 'cape-bone-lcd-00A0.dtbo

bone-capemgr bone_capemgr.9: slot #7: Requesting firmware 'cape-bone-lcd-
00A0.dtbo' for board-name 'Override Board Name', version '00A0'

bone-capemgr bone_capemgr.9: slot #7: dtbo 'cape-bone-lcd-00A0.dtbo'
loaded; converting to live tree

bone-capemgr bone_capemgr.9: slot #7: cape-bone-lcd conflict P9.25
(#5:BB-BONELT-HDMI)

bone-capemgr bone_capemgr.9: slot #7: Failed verification
```

Yes, as stated earlier, we are trying to use the `spi1` bus, which is already used by the HDMI support, so we have to disable it. To do this, we must edit the U-Boot settings in the `/boot/uboot/uEnv.txt` file, and then enable the following line by uncommenting it:

```
optargs=capemgr.disable_partno=BB-BONELT-HDMI,BB-BONELT-HDMIN
```

Then, we only have to reboot the system. Now, if everything was done correctly, we should be able to execute the preceding command without any errors:

```
root@BeagleBone:~# echo cape-bone-lcd > /sys/devices/bone_capemgr.9/slots
root@BeagleBone:~#
```

Great, no errors! In fact, the kernel messages are as follows:

```
[   97.730983] bone-capemgr bone_capemgr.9: part_number 'cape-bone-lcd',
version 'N/A'

[   97.731171] bone-capemgr bone_capemgr.9: slot #7: generic override

[   97.731221] bone-capemgr bone_capemgr.9: bone: Using override eeprom
data at slot 7

[   97.731273] bone-capemgr bone_capemgr.9: slot #7: 'Override Board
Name,00A0,Override Manuf,cape-bone-lcd'

[   97.733684] bone-capemgr bone_capemgr.9: slot #7: Requesting part
number/version based 'cape-bone-lcd-00A0.dtbo

[   97.733746] bone-capemgr bone_capemgr.9: slot #7: Requesting firmware
'cape-bone-lcd-00A0.dtbo' for board-name 'Override Board Name', version
'00A0'

[   97.739277] bone-capemgr bone_capemgr.9: slot #7: dtbo 'cape-bone-lcd-
00A0.dtbo' loaded; converting to live tree

[   97.742132] bone-capemgr bone_capemgr.9: slot #7: #5 overlays

[   97.753265] ehrpwm 48304200.ehrpwm: unable to select pin group

[   97.804760] edma-dma-engine edma-dma-engine.0: allocated channel for
0:43

[   97.804930] edma-dma-engine edma-dma-engine.0: allocated channel for
0:42

[   97.805703] of_get_named_gpio_flags exited with status 115

[   97.805955] of_get_named_gpio_flags exited with status 117

[   99.993676] Console: switching to colour frame buffer device 32x26

[   99.994041] fb0: ST7735 frame buffer device,

[   99.994041]     using 40960 KiB of video memory

[   99.998333] pwm-backlight adafruit-tft-backlight.12: invalid default
brightness level: 101, using 100

[  100.001158] bone-capemgr bone_capemgr.9: slot #7: Applied #5 overlays.
```

In the preceding output, we can see that the BeagleBone Black has enabled a color frame buffer device of `32x26` characters wide that is represented in the user space by the `/dev/fb0` device.

To test our new display, we can try to write some noise into it using the following command:

```
root@BeagleBone:~# cat /dev/urandom > /dev/fb0
cat: write error: No space left on device
```

 You can safely ignore the write error because the `/dev/fb0` device has a fixed size (which is the size of the display area), while the `cat` command would indefinitely read from the `/dev/urandom` device (the random numbers' generator).

The output on the LCD should look something like this:

We have not only got a graphical display, but a terminal too. In fact, we can send some characters to it. Let's clean the screen with the following command:

```
root@BeagleBone:~# cat /dev/zero > /dev/fb0
cat: write error: No space left on device
```

Then, we can write some testing strings to it using these commands:

```
root@BeagleBone:~# echo TEST STRING 1 > /dev/tty0
root@BeagleBone:~# echo TEST STRING 2 > /dev/tty0
root@BeagleBone:~# echo TEST STRING 3 > /dev/tty0
```

On the display, we should now see the preceding strings, one per line.

As a last example, let's try to install the `fim` package, which stores a program that can render a picture on a generic frame buffer device:

`root@BeagleBone:~# aptitude install fim`

Now I can display my social profile on the LCD using the following command:

`root@BeagleBone:~# fim photo-2015.jpg`

Great! The output is shown in the following image:

Notice that my picture is in the *Avatar mode* (the bluish effect); this is because on my device, the SRGB pin of the ST7735 chip (which manages the LCD) is not set correctly. A solution is reported in the following patch:

```
--- a/drivers/video/st7735fb.c
+++ b/drivers/video/st7735fb.c
@@ -72,7 +72,7 @@ static struct st7735_function
st7735_cfg_script[] = {
        { ST7735_DATA, 0x0e},
        { ST7735_CMD, ST7735_INVOFF},
        { ST7735_CMD, ST7735_MADCTL},
-       { ST7735_DATA, 0xc8},
+       { ST7735_DATA, 0xc0},
        { ST7735_CMD, ST7735_COLMOD},
        { ST7735_DATA, 0x05},
        { ST7735_CMD, ST7735_CASET},
```

After applying the patch, you must recompile the driver (or the whole kernel if the driver is statically linked), and then reboot the system.

# Accessing the raw bus

As for the USB and I²C buses, the SPI bus supports the raw access in order to directly send and receive messages from the SPI slaves, so it's time to show you an example on how we can do it on our BeagleBone Black.

We are going to manage a really simple device: the thermocouple to digital converter, as shown in the following image:

 The device can be purchased at (or by surfing the Internet) http://www.cosino.io/product/thermocouple-max31855.

By looking at the chip's datasheet at the URL http://datasheets.maximintegrated.com/en/ds/MAX31855.pdf, we can see that its functioning is very simple: it has one 32-bit register, where we can read the temperature information. The register has the following format:

| 14-bit thermocouple data | | | | Res | Fault | 12-bit internal temperature | | | | Res | SCV | SCG | OC |
|------|------|-----|------|------|------|------|------|-----|------|------|------|------|------|
| D31 | D30 | ... | D18 | D17 | D16 | D15 | D14 | ... | D4 | D3 | D2 | D1 | D0 |
| Sign | MSB | X | LSB | - | X | X | MSB | X | LSB | - | X | X | X |

So, in order to read the temperature data, we have to read the preceding register and extract the datum from the bits D30-D18. Note that we should also check the bit D16 in order to know whether the peripheral is in a faulting state or not.

Note that D30 corresponds to the value $2^{10}$, while D18 corresponds to $2^{-2}$, so the datum in the bits D30-D18 must be divided by 4 to get the real temperature data.

You can notice that this chip can give us more information, but I decided to keep my example as simple as possible, but, of course, you can improve it to fully retrieve all the needed information.

Recall what we did at the beginning of this chapter - we have to create the SPI bus device to use in order to get access to the sensor. However, we cannot use the /lib/firmware/BB-SPIDEV0-00A0.dtbo file, as the chip works at 5 MHz maximum frequency, and while in the file, this parameter is set to 16 MHz. To verify this, and in order to get a human-readable form of the SPI settings, we can use the dtc program as follows:

```
root@BeagleBone:~# dtc -O dts -I dtb /lib/firmware/BB-SPIDEV0-00A0.dtbo >
BB-SPIDEV0-00A0.dts
```

The generated file is reported in chapter_09/BB-SPIDEV0-1M-00A0. dts in the book's example code repository.

In this file, we can safely drop the channel@1 section since we have no devices connected to it, and we can fix the bus' maximum frequency by modifying the spi-max-frequency entry. Here, the patch against the original file is as follows:

```
root@BeagleBone:~# diff -u BB-SPIDEV0-00A0.dts BB-SPIDEV0-1M-00A0.dts
--- BB-SPIDEV0-00A0.dts      2014-04-23 21:28:12.736328295 +0000
+++ BB-SPIDEV0-1M-00A0.dts   2014-04-23 20:34:16.324218852 +0000
@@ -34,17 +34,9 @@
                     #size-cells = <0x0>;
                     compatible = "spidev";
                     reg = <0x0>;
-                    spi-max-frequency = <0xf42400>;
+                    spi-max-frequency = <1000000>;
                     spi-cpha;
             };
-
-             channel@1 {
-                     #address-cells = <0x1>;
-                     #size-cells = <0x0>;
```

```
-                             compatible = "spidev";
-                             reg = <0x1>;
-                             spi-max-frequency = <0xf42400>;
-                    };
          };
     };
```

Then, we should change the name of the file in BB-SPIDEV0-1M-00A0.dts in order to create our own settings. Now, the new firmware file is created, again, using the dtc command:

```
root@BeagleBone:~# dtc -O dtb -o /lib/firmware/BB-SPIDEV0-1M-00A0.dtbo -b
0 -@ BB-SPIDEV0-1M-00A0.dts
```

Then, we can load it using the usual command:

```
root@BeagleBone:~# echo BB-SPIDEV0-1M > /sys/devices/bone_capemgr.9/slots
```

The SPI device is now ready to be used:

```
root@BeagleBone:~# ls /dev/spidev*
/dev/spidev1.0
```

Now we must complete the electrical connections, so in the following table, I reported the correspondence between the BeagleBone Black's pins and the thermocouple board's pins:

| BeagleBone Black pins – label | Thermocouple board pins – label |
| --- | --- |
| P9.4 – VCC | 6 – VCC |
| P9.21 – MISO | 3 – Serial data output |
| P9.18 – MOSI | Not connected |
| P9.22 – SCLK | 4 – Clock |
| P9.17 – SS0 | 1 – Chip select |
| P9.2 – GND | 5 – GND |

The code to read the thermocouple data is reported in chapter_09/spi_thermo/ spi_thermo.c in the book's example code repository.

Note that we simply open() the /dev/spidev1.0 SPI device file, and then we do a read(). The remaining code is just for decoding the data read. The snippet of the relevant code is given as follows:

```
/* Open the SPI bus device connected to the thermocouple chip */
fd = open(SPI_DEV, O_RDWR);
```

```
if (fd < 0) {
        fprintf(stderr, "%s: cannot get access to SPI bus\n", NAME);
        exit(1);
}

/* Read the 32-bt data */
ret = read(fd, &data, 4);
if (ret < 0) {
        fprintf(stderr, "%s: cannot read data from SPI device\n", NAME);
        exit(1);
}
if (ret != 4) {
        fprintf(stderr, "%s: short read\n", NAME);
        exit(1);
}
```

Now we can compile the code using the make command as usual. If everything works well, we can read the environment temperature using the following command:

```
root@BeagleBone:~# ./spi_thermo
18.50
```

# Summary

As you can see the SPI bus is quite powerful, as it implements an efficient data stream; on the other hand, it can be easily managed with a large variety of different slave devices.

In the next chapter, we'll see another available bus for our BeagleBone Black that allows us to communicate with some sensors using only one wire. It's time to go to the next chapter and discover the 1-Wire bus.

# 10
# 1-Wire Bus – W1

After looking at the most frequently used buses that a developer can find on an embedded computer (USB, I²C, and SPI), it's time to present a less famous, but not less important, communication bus: the **1-Wire bus** (called one-wire and usually abbreviated as **W1** or **OW**).

Even if this bus is quite slow with respect to other buses, it's interesting because it permits users to communicate with a remote device using only one wire. This allows you to simplify the connections between the CPU and its peripherals, giving the designer the possibility to have the most economical and simple way to add electronic devices for identification, authentication, and delivery of calibration data or manufacturing information to a computer board.

## What is the 1-Wire bus?

The 1-Wire bus is a half-duplex and asynchronous GND. However, despite this feature, most devices have three wires: the data signal, GND, and power supply (VCC).

 Let me remind you that half-duplex communication can transmit and receive but not at the same time on the bus (the data can flow in one direction only) while asynchronous means that no clock is sent along with the data.

When a device has two wires only, it must include an in-built energy storage mechanism (usually a capacitor) to store the charge to power itself during periods when the data is really exchanged; that is, the device takes its power from the data pin instead of the regular power pin, and due to this, this functioning method is called **parasite mode**.

The drawback of this feature is that communication with these kind of devices is slower. In fact, as shown in the following diagram, in the parasite mode, the data line must be pulled high prior to the beginning of the data transfer, for an amount of time sufficient to charge the internal capacitor on the device. When the capacitor is charged, it can power the device to permit the data exchange:

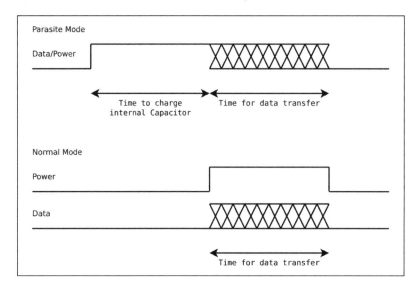

On a 1-Wire bus, there is always one master, which typically is a microcontroller, and several slaves. The master initiates each communication activity on the bus, so that the slaves can only act when addressed. Each slave has a unique 64-bit serial number that the master uses to address a well-defined device over the bus.

Since the slaves addresses are not known by the master, it uses an enumeration protocol (a particular broadcast message) to discover all the connected devices called **singulation**. Once all the devices are detected, the master can send a selection command with the address of a particular device, so that the next command is executed only by the addressed device.

What is very interesting of this bus is that every single slave can be disconnected and then reconnected without any problems for both the slave and the master; in fact, the master can detect a new slave and also discover when a slave has been removed. On the other side, a slave can store its configuration in a nonvolatile memory, and start to work again as soon as it is reconnected to the bus.

The details on how the 1-Wire bus works is out of the scope of this book. You can check out this URL for more information at `http://en.wikipedia.org/wiki/1-Wire`.

# The electrical lines

The 1-Wire bus lines are reported in the following table:

| Name | Description |
|------|-------------|
| data: Data (and power when no VCC) | This is the bus data signal |
| GND | This is the common ground |
| VCC (optional) | This is the optional power supply |

In the case of there being multiple devices connected, they must be connected in parallel, as shown in the following diagram:

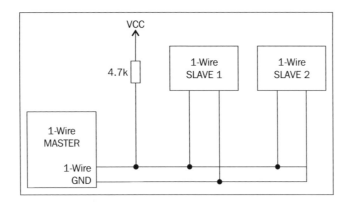

 Note that the 4.7K resistor must be added in order to allow the sensor to work otherwise we'll have no communication at all!

# The 1-Wire bus in Linux

On our BeagleBone Black, there are no 1-Wire controllers, so we have to find a way to implement one in order to be able to talk to a 1-Wire device. Several solutions exist but considering the low data transfer of this bus, the best and cheapest option is to use a software solution.

In Linux, several buses can be emulated by the software and the 1-Wire bus (along with the I²C and SPI buses) is one of them. In order to do so, we need to locate the driver, in Linux's sources, in the `drivers/w1/masters/w1-gpio.c` file, and we simply need to choose a GPIO, which is to be selected as the data bus, and the trick is done.

The DTS file used to set up the BeagleBone Black and the `w1-gpio` driver can be written in the `chapter_10/BB-W1-GPIO-00A0.dts` file in the book's example code repository. In this file, the pin **P8.11** is used as a data signal, and in `fragment@0`, there is the related GPIO setup:

```
/* Define the pins usage */
exclusive-use =
        /* the pin header P8 uses */
        "P8.11",
        /* Hardware IP cores in use */
        "gpio1_13";

fragment@0 {
        target = <&am33xx_pinmux>;

        __overlay__ {
                bb_w1_pins: pinmux_bb_w1_pins {
                        pinctrl-single,pins = <0x34 0x37>;
                };
        };
};
```

Recall what we said in the *Getting access to SPI devices* section of *Chapter 9, Serial Peripheral Interface – SPI*, about the GPIO settings. We can verify in the file (at `https://github.com/derekmolloy/boneDeviceTree/blob/master/docs/BeagleboneBlackP8HeaderTable.pdf`) that the two magic numbers in the `pinctrl-single,pins` line represent the pin offset and setting respectively, which enable the internal pull-up, as requested by the 1-Wire bus.

In `fragment@1`, we instruct the `w1-gpio` driver which pin it must use in order to emulate our 1-Wire controller. The relative code snippet is as follows:

```
fragment@1 {
        target = <&ocp>;

        __overlay__ {
                #address-cells  = <1>;
                #size-cell      = <0>;
                status          = "okay";

                /* Setup the pins */
```

```
        pinctrl-names    = "default";
        pinctrl-0        = <&bb_w1_pins>;

        /* Define the new one-wire master as based on w1-gpio
         * and using GPIO1_13
         */
        onewire@0 {
                compatible    = "w1-gpio";
                gpios         = <&gpio2 13 0>;
        };
    };
};
```

Now, to enable the 1-Wire controller emulator, we have to first compile the code with the usual command:

```
root@BeagleBone:~# dtc -O dtb -o /lib/firmware/BB-W1-GPIO-00A0.dtbo -b 0
-@ BB-W1-GPIO-00A0.dts
```

Then, enable the driver using the following command:

```
root@BeagleBone:~# echo BB-W1-GPIO > /sys/devices/bone_capemgr.9/slots
```

If everything works well, the following kernel activities should be read in the kernel messages:

```
bone-capemgr bone_capemgr.9: part_number 'BB-W1-GPIO', version 'N/A'

bone-capemgr bone_capemgr.9: slot #7: generic override

bone-capemgr bone_capemgr.9: bone: Using override eeprom data at slot 7

bone-capemgr bone_capemgr.9: slot #7: 'Override Board Name,00A0,Override
Manuf,BB-W1-GPIO'

bone-capemgr bone_capemgr.9: slot #7: Requesting part number/version
based 'BB-W1-GPIO-00A0.dtbo

bone-capemgr bone_capemgr.9: slot #7: Requesting firmware 'BB-W1-GPIO-
00A0.dtbo' for board-name 'Override Board Name', version '00A0'

bone-capemgr bone_capemgr.9: slot #7: dtbo 'BB-W1-GPIO-00A0.dtbo' loaded;
converting to live tree

bone-capemgr bone_capemgr.9: slot #7: #2 overlays

w1-gpio onewire@0.12: unable to select pin group

of_get_named_gpio_flags exited with status 45

of_get_named_gpio_flags: can't parse gpios property

bone-capemgr bone_capemgr.9: slot #7: Applied #2 overlays.
```

On the sysfs filesystem, we should get the following output:

```
root@BeagleBone:~# ls -l /sys/bus/w1/devices/
total 0
lrwxrwxrwx 1 root root 0 Apr 25 12:49 w1_bus_master1 -> ../../../devices/w1_bus_master1
```

Obviously, we get no devices at all since we still have no 1-Wire devices connected to our new bus. So, let's go to the next section, and let's start managing a 1-Wire device with our BeagleBone Black.

# Getting access to 1-Wire devices

To show you how the 1-Wire bus works, we can use a really simple chip: the temperature sensor chip DS18B20. There are two possible ways or modes by which the chip can be powered: a parasite version (that is, which works in the parasite mode), with two wires only, and a normal version with a dedicated power pin, which uses the three wires instead.

In this example, I'm going to use the three wire's waterproof version of this chip, which implements a special packaging of the chip that can be used in hostile environments (see the following figure for the images of the two chip's packaging version):

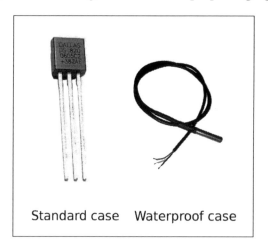

Standard case    Waterproof case

 The device can be purchased at (or by surfing the Internet) http://www.cosino.io/product/waterproof-temperature-sensor.

First of all, we've to set up the electrical connections. In the following table, the correspondence between the BeagleBone Black's pins and the sensor's cables is reported:

| BeagleBone Black pins – label | Sensor cables – Color / Standard case pin |
| --- | --- |
| P9.4 – **VCC** | Red / rightmost pin |
| P8.11 | White / center pin |
| P9.2 – **GND** | Black / leftmost pin |

 Even if it's not strictly needed to understand what we're going to do, the chip's datasheet is available at the URL `http://datasheets.maximintegrated.com/en/ds/DS18B20.pdf`.

Once connected, the sensor is automatically detected, and it should be listed in the `/sys/bus/w1/devices/` directory, as shown in the following snippet:

```
root@BeagleBone:~# ls -l /sys/bus/w1/devices/
total 0
lrwxrwxrwx 1 root root 0 Feb 14 19:16 28-000004b541e9 -> ../../../devices/w1_bus_
master1/28-000004b541e9
lrwxrwxrwx 1 root root 0 Feb 14 19:16 w1_bus_master1 -> ../../../devices/w1_bus_master1
```

In the preceding output, we can see that our sensor has the 1-Wire ID set to `28-000004b541e9`. Note that in the case of multiple 1-Wire buses, we can discover where they are connected by looking at each controller's directory, as displayed in the following snippet:

```
root@BeagleBone:~# ls -l /sys/bus/w1/devices/w1_bus_master1/
total 0
drwxr-xr-x 3 root root    0 Feb 14 19:16 28-000004b541e9
lrwxrwxrwx 1 root root    0 Feb 14 19:18 driver -> ../../bus/w1/drivers/
w1_master_driver
drwxr-xr-x 2 root root    0 Feb 14 19:18 power
lrwxrwxrwx 1 root root    0 Feb 14 19:11 subsystem -> ../../bus/w1
-rw-r--r-- 1 root root 4096 Feb 14 19:11 uevent
-rw-rw-r-- 1 root root 4096 Feb 14 19:18 w1_master_add
-r--r--r-- 1 root root 4096 Feb 14 19:18 w1_master_attempts
-r--r--r-- 1 root root 4096 Feb 14 19:18 w1_master_max_slave_count
-r--r--r-- 1 root root 4096 Feb 14 19:18 w1_master_name
```

```
-r--r--r-- 1 root root 4096 Feb 14 19:18 w1_master_pointer
-rw-rw-r-- 1 root root 4096 Feb 14 19:18 w1_master_pullup
-rw-rw-r-- 1 root root 4096 Feb 14 19:18 w1_master_remove
-rw-rw-r-- 1 root root 4096 Feb 14 19:18 w1_master_search
-r--r--r-- 1 root root 4096 Feb 14 19:18 w1_master_slave_count
-r--r--r-- 1 root root 4096 Feb 14 19:18 w1_master_slaves
-r--r--r-- 1 root root 4096 Feb 14 19:18 w1_master_timeout
```

Obviously, our controller's name is `w1_bus_master1`, and the files are all related to it in the same directory. For instance, in the `w1_master_slave_count` and `w1_master_slaves` files, we can find how many slaves have been detected by the controller and the corresponding slaves list respectively:

```
root@BeagleBone:~# cat /sys/bus/w1/devices/w1_bus_master1/w1_master_
slave_count
1
root@BeagleBone:~# cat /sys/bus/w1/devices/w1_bus_master1/w1_master_
slaves
28-000004b541e9
```

Ok, now we can come back to our temperature sensor. In order to get the temperature's environment, we can take a look at the slave's directory:

```
root@BeagleBone:~# ls -l /sys/bus/w1/devices/28-000004b541e9/
total 0
lrwxrwxrwx 1 root root    0 Feb 14 19:17 driver -> ../../../bus/w1/
drivers/w1_slave_driver
-r--r--r-- 1 root root 4096 Feb 14 19:17 id
-r--r--r-- 1 root root 4096 Feb 14 19:17 name
drwxr-xr-x 2 root root    0 Feb 14 19:17 power
lrwxrwxrwx 1 root root    0 Feb 14 19:16 subsystem -> ../../../bus/w1
-rw-r--r-- 1 root root 4096 Feb 14 19:16 uevent
-r--r--r-- 1 root root 4096 Feb 14 19:17 w1_slave
```

In the `id` file, we can read the device's ID in a raw binary format:

```
root@BeagleBone:~# od -tx1 /sys/bus/w1/devices/28-000004b541e9/id
0000000 28 e9 41 b5 04 00 00 0b
0000010
```

While in the `name` file, we will read the device's ID as a string:

```
root@BeagleBone:~# cat /sys/bus/w1/devices/28-000004b541e9/name
28-000004b541e9
```

However, the file we wish to get (where we can find the temperature) is `w1_slave`. In fact, if we read it, we get the following output:

```
root@BeagleBone:~# cat /sys/bus/w1/devices/28-000004b541e9/w1_slave
48 01 00 04 1f ff 08 10 da : crc=da YES
48 01 00 04 1f ff 08 10 da t=20500
```

The desired temperature is then `20500`, which is in $m°C$, that is, 20.5°C.

# Summary

In this chapter, we discovered the 1-Wire bus and how it can be used in order to get data from a simple temperature sensor device. Also, in the course of the previous few chapters, we went through a variety of communication protocols and saw how to connect common hardware peripherals to the BeagleBone Black.

Now that we know how to collect data from several devices, in the last chapter of this book, we will see how to write a dedicated software that constantly executes a controlling/monitoring procedure. In the next chapter, we are going to present the system daemons.

# 11
# Useful System Daemons

In the previous chapters, I presented you with several peripherals, and we saw how they can be connected with the BeagleBone Black, just to demonstrate how this board can be versatile and expandable. However, having the possibility to communicate with several devices is just the first step to getting a fully functional monitoring system.

The main target of a system, with so many devices connected to it, is to control or monitor these devices, and to do so, it needs a dedicated software which constantly executes a controlling/monitoring procedure. This kind of software is usually called a **daemon**.

In Unix terminology, a daemon is a computer program that runs as a background process, rather than being under the direct control of an interactive user, so they are perfect to execute a controlling/monitoring procedure.

In this last chapter, we're going to show you how an embedded developer can use existing daemons or a newly written daemon in several programming languages.

## What is a daemon?

As already stated, a daemon is a computer program that runs as a background process. In particular, for an Unix system, the Unix Bible, *Advanced Programming in the UNIX Environment*, *Addison-Wesley*, by Richard Stevens says:

> *Daemons are processes that live for a long time. They are often started when the system is bootstrapped and terminate only when the system is shutdown. We say they run in background, because they don't have a controlling terminal.*

This behavior is so important that a special function has been implemented in the glibc library that permits the developer to easily create a **daemon process**. The function is (obviously) named daemon().

You can see its documentation using the following command on every GNU/Linux system:

```
$ man daemon
```

Just to fix this concept, let's take a look at a possible implementation of the daemon() function in order to show you which steps a process should perform to turn itself into a daemon:

```c
int daemon(void)
{
    int fd;

    /* Create the daemon grand-child process */
    switch (fork()) {
    case -1:
            return -1;    /* error! */
    case 0:
            break;        /* child continues... */
    default:
            exit(0);      /* parent goes... bye bye!! */
    }

    /* This code is now executed by the shell's grand-child */

    if (setsid() < 0)          /* become a session leader */
            return -1;

    if (chdir("/") < 0)        /* change working directory */
            return -1;

    umask(0);                  /* clear file mode creation mask */

    /* In the end close all open file descriptors */
    for (fd = sysconf(_SC_OPEN_MAX); fd > 0; fd--)
            close(fd);

    return 0;
}
```

The first thing to do for a daemon candidate process is to call the fork() system call and then the exit() system call. This is because if the daemon has started as a simple shell command, then to have the parent terminate makes the shell think that the command is done and that the prompt can be returned to the user. Then, the setsid() call is needed to run the new daemon candidate process in a new session and to have no controlling terminal.

The chdir() system call is needed in order to avoid the daemon candidate process that runs on a mounted filesystem, and prevent it from being unmounted. In fact, the current working directory is inherited by the parent, and changing this to the root (the slash character "/" in the preceding code) is a trick to prevent this problem. The umask() system call is then used to permit the newly-created daemon to create files with specific permissions without restrictions.

The last step closes all the open file descriptors eventually inherited by the grandparent (in this case, the shell). By closing all the process communication channels, the daemon cannot be managed by the user anymore. However, in order to make this possible, to change some daemon's functionalities, it may reopen a dedicated channel (usually a Unix domain socket), where it can receive some configuration commands, or it can be designed in such a way to reread its configuration file when a special signal arrives. Details of how a daemon works or how it can be created is out of the scope of this book. You can take a look at http://en.wikipedia.org/wiki/Daemon_%28computing%29 or (better) read the Unix Bible, *Advanced Programming in the UNIX Environment*, *Addison-Wesley*, by Richard Stevens.

# Useful and ready-to-use daemons

In a GNU/Linux system, (in general, a Unix system), there exists a lot of ready-to-use daemons used to do real common tasks. The most notable are:

- **Apache and other similar tools**: These are the **Hypertext Transfer Protocol (HTTP)** server daemons
- **atd and crond**: These are the task scheduler daemons
- **inetd and xinetd**: These are the Internet super server daemons
- **named/bind and other similar tools**: These are the **Domain Name System (DNS)** server daemons
- **nfsd, lockd, mountd, and statd**: These are the **Network File System (NFS)** daemon and support daemons
- **ntpd**: This is the **Network Time Protocol (NTP)** service daemon
- **portmap and rpcbind**: These are SunRPC port mappers
- **mysqld, postgresql, and other similar tools**: These are the database server daemons
- **sendmail, exim, postfix, and other similar tools**: These are mail transfer agent daemons

- **snmpd**: This is the simple network management protocol daemon
- **syslogd and other similar tools**: These are the system logging daemons
- **systemd**: This is the system management daemon
- **telnetd and sshd**: These are telnet and secure shell server daemons
- **vsftpd and other similar tools**: These are the **File Transfer Protocol (FTP)** server daemons

Some of them have already been introduced in the previous chapters. As they have been used in some examples, I'm going to add a little list of other useful daemons that the developer can use to simplify his/her job with a brief explanation on how to use and get access to them.

For the other daemons, let me encourage you to surf the Internet in order to know more about them; you may discover interesting things.

# Syslogd

When we talk about daemons, one of the most important ones is **syslogd**. The syslogd is a widely used standard for message logging that permits the separation of the software that generates messages, the system that stores them, and the software that reports and analyzes them.

Because a daemon has by default all the communication channels closed, this is the most efficient and easier method to report a daemon activity to the system administrator/developer.

## Using in Bash

In our BeagleBone Black board, the syslogd is already set up and running, and it can be used in several ways. From the Bash shell, we can use the `logger` command as follows:

```
root@BeagleBone:~# logger -t mydaemon logging message in bash
```

This command will generate the following message in the `/var/log/syslog` file:

```
root@BeagleBone:~# tail -f /var/log/syslog | grep mydaemon
Mar  6 15:25:14 BeagleBone mydaemon: logging message in bash
```

# Using in C

The same message can also be generated in C language using the code in the `chapter_11/syslogd/logger.c` file in the book's example code repository. The code simply calls the three functions to do its job, and the code snippet is as follows:

```
openlog("mydaemon", LOG_NOWAIT, LOG_USER);

syslog(LOG_INFO, "logging message in C");
closelog();
```

Just compile and execute it using the following command lines:

**root@BeagleBone:~# make logger**

**root@BeagleBone:~# ./logger**

In the `/var/log/syslog` file, we should get the following output:

**Mar  6 15:30:53 BeagleBone mydaemon: logging message in C**

# Using in PHP

In PHP, we can use the code in the `chapter_11/syslogd/logger.php` file in the book's example code repository. Again, we just need three functions to do the job. The code snippet is as follows:

```
openlog("mydaemon", LOG_NOWAIT, LOG_USER);
syslog(LOG_INFO, "logging message in PHP");
closelog();
```

The example program can be executed with the following command:

**root@BeagleBone:# php logger.php**

The generated message is:

**Mar  6 15:34:15 BeagleBone mydaemon: logging message in PHP**

# Using in Python

The last example is in Python, and it's stored in the `chapter_11/syslogd/logger.py` file in the book's example code repository. We will again use the same three functions:

```
syslog.openlog("mydaemon", syslog.LOG_NOWAIT, syslog.LOG_USER)
syslog.syslog(syslog.LOG_INFO, "logging message in Python")
syslog.closelog()
```

We will execute the following command:

```
root@BeagleBone:~# python logger.py
```

This should generate the following message:

```
Mar  6 15:38:56 BeagleBone mydaemon: logging message in Python
```

# Cron

This daemon is very useful to execute simple and repetitive tasks in the background; in fact, it executes the scheduled shell commands according to a timetable called **crontab**, which the developer can use to program his/her tasks.

The crontab must be accessed and updated using the crontab command, and in order to better explain how the cron daemon works, you should take a look at the current crontab of the BeagleBone Black's root user using the following command:

```
root@BeagleBone:~# crontab -e
```

When the preceding command is used, the BeagleBone Black will open a text file, using the current text editor, where the content is shown as follows:

```
# Edit this file to introduce tasks to be run by cron.
#
# Each task to run has to be defined through a single line
# indicating with different fields when the task will be run
# and what command to run for the task
#
# To define the time you can provide concrete values for
# minute (m), hour (h), day of month (dom), month (mon),
# and day of week (dow) or use '*' in these fields (for 'any').#
# Notice that tasks will be started based on the cron's system
# daemon's notion of time and timezones.
#
# Output of the crontab jobs (including errors) is sent through
# email to the user the crontab file belongs to (unless redirected).
#
# For example, you can run a backup of all your user accounts
# at 5 a.m every week with:
# 0 5 * * 1 tar -zcf /var/backups/home.tgz /home/
#
# For more information see the manual pages of crontab(5) and cron(8)
#
# m h  dom mon dow    command
```

Note that the default editor can be changed by setting the EDITOR environment variable as follows:

```
root@BeagleBone:~# EDITOR=vim
```

Then, the BeagleBone Black will use the vim command to show the file that stores the crontab command.

It's quite easy to understand how the daemon works by just reading the comments in the crontab file. We have one task per line, and the first five fields of each line define at which instance the command in the sixth field must be executed. For example, as reported in the preceding comments, to run a backup of all the BeagleBone Black's user accounts at 5 a.m. every week, the schedule line should be as follows:

```
0 5 * * 1 tar -zcf /var/backups/home.tgz /home/
```

The first five fields do the trick; in fact, the first field tells cron that the command must be run at 0 minutes (m), the second sets the execution hour (h) at 5 (hours are from 0 to 23), the third and the fourth fields, using the wildcard * character, respectively tell that the command must be executed on each day of the month (dom) and each month (mon), while the fifth field tells that the command must be executed on the day of week (dow) 1, that is, on Monday (numbers 0 or 7 is for Sunday).

Another useful feature is that in the crontab file, the developer can also set some variables to modify the default behavior; for example, the default value for the PATH variable is /usr/bin:/bin, and you can modify it to add the user's bin directory using the following command line:

```
PATH=~/bin:/usr/bin/:/bin
```

Note that the character ~ is correctly interpreted by the shell (which by default is set to SHELL=/bin/bash), while the same is not valid for the environmental substitutions or replacement of variables, and thus, the following line will not work as you might expect, that is, there will not be any substitution:

```
PATH = $HOME/bin:$PATH
```

# MySQL

Usually, we consider this daemon to be used on large servers, but it can be efficiently used in an embedded system too. For example, it can be used to implement a common configuration system, or a status system, where more processes can get/set the configuration data and/or status data. Or it can also be used efficiently to log several events and/or environment's data collected from the sensors.

In the *MySQL* section under *The LAMP suite* of *Chapter 1, Installing the Developing System*, we set up this daemon, so now we can see several ways to get access to its internals. From Bash, we can use the `mysql` command, as shown in the following snippet:

```
root@BeagleBone:~/mysql# mysql -u root -p
Enter password:
Welcome to the MySQL monitor.  Commands end with ; or \g.
Your MySQL connection id is 38
Server version: 5.5.38-0+wheezy1 (Debian)

Copyright (c) 2000, 2014, Oracle and/or its affiliates. All rights reserved.

Oracle is a registered trademark of Oracle Corporation and/or its
affiliates. Other names may be trademarks of their respective owners.

Type 'help;' or '\h' for help. Type '\c' to clear the current input
statement.

mysql>
```

Note that when the BeagleBone Black asks for a password, I just use the one I set up in the *MySQL* section under *The LAMP suite* of *Chapter 1, Installing the Developing System*.

## Getting access in Bash

To use MySQL efficiently, we should create a custom database, and then use it to do our job. For example, we can use the script in the `chapter_11/mysql/my_init.sh` file in the book's example code repository to generate a custom database called `sproject`.

The code is quite simple: after a warning message, we use the `__EOF__` trick used in the *MySQL* section under *The LAMP suite* of *Chapter 1, Installing the Developing System*, to pass a script from the command line to the `mysql` tool. The script first recreates a new database (eventually deleting all the existing data), and then adds a new status table that we can use to store a system's status data. Here is the code snippet:

```
# Drop all existing data!!!
DROP DATABASE IF EXISTS sproject;

# Create new database
CREATE DATABASE sproject;

# Grant privileges
```

```
GRANT USAGE ON *.* TO user@localhost IDENTIFIED BY 'userpass';
GRANT ALL PRIVILEGES ON sproject.* TO user@localhost;
FLUSH PRIVILEGES;

# Select database
USE sproject;

# Create the statuses table
CREATE TABLE status (
    t DATETIME NOT NULL,
    n VARCHAR(64) NOT NULL,
    v VARCHAR(64) NOT NULL,
    PRIMARY KEY (n),
    INDEX (n)
) ENGINE=MEMORY;
```

Note that the table has been created using the MEMORY engine. This engine uses the system's memory to store the information instead of using the mass memory devices (for example, hard disks, microSD cards, and so on). This trick allow us to execute very quick queries to the database, but it can be used where the data is dynamically recreated each time our system restarts, as they vanish at the system reboot (also, we must consider that the maximum size of the database is limited by the amount of the installed memory).

At this point, we can add some entries using the code in the chapter_11/mysql/my_ set.sh file in the book's example code repository. We can use it with the following command line:

**root@BeagleBone:# ./my_set.sh T1 23.5**

The script uses the REPLACE SQL command to do its job. The code snippet is just a line of code, which is as follows:

```
REPLACE INTO status (t, n, v) VALUES(now(), '$name', '$value');
```

Now, to verify that the data is correctly collected in the database, we can do a simple dump of the status table created earlier, using the chapter_11/mysql/my_init.sh file in the book's example code repository. Then, we use the following command to dump all of the data into the table:

**root@BeagleBone:~# ./my_dump.sh**

**t      n       v**

**2015-03-06 16:30:27     T1      23.5**

In this case, the job is done using the SELECT SQL command. Again, the code snippet is just a line of code:

```
SELECT * FROM status;
```

The real power of MySQL is that earlier actions can be done in different languages, and, just to give you some useful hints, you can start developing its controlling/monitoring system with the BeagleBone Black. I'm going to show you how to get access to the sproject database from C, PHP, and Python languages.

 Note that in the next example, I'm not going to rewrite the my_init. sh script in different languages, since it can be deduced from the other examples. In any case, it is not a significant example. It just creates the database and, once used, it is not useful anymore.

# Getting access in C

In C language, the my_set script can be implemented in the chapter_11/mysql/my_set.c file in the book's example code repository. The code is quite similar to the one in Bash, even if it is a bit complex. However, the important parts are the three calls to the mysql_init(), mysql_real_connect(), and mysql_query() functions. The first two just initiate the connection, while the third function executes the query. Here is the code snippet:

```
/* Get connect to MySQL daemon */
c = mysql_init(NULL);
if (!c) {
        fprintf(stderr, "unable to init MySQL data struct\n");
        return -1;
}

if (!mysql_real_connect(c, "127.0.0.1", "user", "userpass",
                        "sproject", 0, NULL, 0)) {
        fprintf(stderr, "unable to connect to MySQL daemon\n");
        ret = -1;
        goto close_db;
}

/* Ok, do the job! */
ret = asprintf(&sql, query, name, value);
if (ret < 0) {
        fprintf(stderr, "unable to allocate memory for query\n");
```

```
        goto close_db;
}

ret = mysql_query(c, sql);
if (ret < 0)
        fprintf(stderr, "unable to access the database\n");
```

To complete our panoramic view, we just have to show how you can retrieve the data from the MySQL daemon; to do so, we just need a simple implementation of the my_dump file, as mentioned in the chapter_11/mysql/my_dump.c file in the book's example code repository. Note that in this case, the first three steps are quite similar with the my_set case, but now we have to manage an answer from the MySQL daemon too. To do so, we use the mysql_store_result() function that stores the received data in the q_res variable, and then using the mysql_fetch_field(), mysql_num_fields(), and mysql_fetch_row() functions, we can extract the needed information. The code snippet of the relevant part is as follows:

```
/* Do the dump of the fields' names */
while ((field = mysql_fetch_field(q_res)))
        printf("%s\t", field->name);
printf("\n");

/* Do the dump one line at time */
n = mysql_num_fields(q_res);
while ((row = mysql_fetch_row(q_res))) {
        for (i = 0; i < n; i++)
                printf("%s\t", row[i] ? row[i] : NULL);
        printf("\n");
}

mysql_free_result(q_res);
```

Well, now we are ready to compile the preceding programs:

```
root@BeagleBone:~# make
cc -Wall -O2 -D_GNU_SOURCE -I/usr/include/mysql my_set.c   -lmysqlclient -o my_set
cc -Wall -O2 -D_GNU_SOURCE -I/usr/include/mysql my_dump.c   -lmysqlclient -o my_dump
```

> Note that by default the libraries needed to compile these C programs are not installed in the BeagleBone Black filesystem, so you should add them using the following command:
>
> ```
> root@BeagleBone:~# aptitude install libmysqlclient-dev
> ```

Then, we can use them as we did earlier with Bash:

```
root@BeagleBone:~# ./my_set T1 20
root@BeagleBone:~# ./my_dump
t      n      v
2015-03-12 19:05:25     T1      20
```

# Getting access in PHP

Now it's the PHP's turn, and the `my_set` program is in the `chapter_11/mysql/my_set.php` file in the book's example code repository. In this case, the code is more compact than in C, but it looks like very similar: we still have a connection stage and then a query execution stage. The involved functions are now `mysql_connect()`, `mysql_select_db()`, and `mysql_query()`. The relevant code is reported in the following snippet:

```php
# Get connect to MySQL daemon
$ret = mysql_connect("127.0.0.1", "user", "userpass");
if (!$ret)
    die("unable to connect with MySQL daemon");

$ret = mysql_select_db("sproject");
if (!$ret)
    die("unable to select database");

# Ok, do the job!
$query = "REPLACE INTO status (t, n, v) " .
    "VALUES(now(), '$name', '$value');";
$dbres = mysql_query($query);
if (!$dbres)
    die("unable to execute the query");
```

As in C, the PHP version of the `my_dump` file has to manage the answer from the MySQL daemon, and the code is in the `chapter_11/mysql/my_dump.php` file in the book's example code repository. Even in this case, after the query, we get some data back, which we can extract using the `mysql_num_fields()`, `mysql_field_name()`, and `mysql_fetch_array()` functions. Here is the code snippet:

```php
# Do the dump of the fields' names
$n = mysql_num_fields($dbres);
for ($i = 0; $i < $n; $i++)
    printf("%s\t", mysql_field_name($dbres, $i));
printf("\n");
```

```
# Do the dump one line at time
while ($row = mysql_fetch_array($dbres)) {
    for ($i = 0; $i < $n; $i++)
        printf("%s\t", $row[$i]);
    printf("\n");
}
```

These programs can now be used as the other programs, as follows:

**root@BeagleBone:~# ./my_set.php T1 19.5**

**root@BeagleBone:~# ./my_dump.php**

```
t     n     v
2015-03-12 19:20:17     T1      19.5
```

# Getting access in Python

In Python, the my_set program can be as it is in the chapter_11/mysql/my_set.py file in the book's example code repository. The program looks a bit different from the previous one due the usage of the cursor. However, if we look carefully at the code, we can see that there are very few differences. The MySQLdb.connect() function does the connection with the MySQL daemon, and the execute() method just executes the query. Here is the code snippet:

```
# Get connect to MySQL daemon
db = MySQLdb.connect(host = "localhost", user = "user", passwd = "userpass",
                     db = "sproject")

# Create the Cursor object to execute all queries
c = db.cursor()

# Ok, do the job!
query = "REPLACE INTO status (t, n, v) " \
    "VALUES(now(), '%s', '%s');" % (sys.argv[1], sys.argv[2])
c.execute(query)
```

The my_dump file can be located in the chapter_11/mysql/my_dump.py file in the book's example code repository. This time, in order to retrieve the query's data, we will use the fetchall() method, and to get the headers, we will use the description attribute. The relevant code is reported in the following snippet:

```
# Save the query result
data = c.fetchall()

# Do the dump of the fields' names
for field in c.description:
    print("%s\t" % (field[0])),
```

```
        print

        # Do the dump one line at time
        n = len(c.description)
        for row in data:
                for i in range(0, n):
                        print("%s\t" % (row[i])),
                print
```

In the end, we can test these programs using the following commands:

**root@BeagleBone:~# ./my_set.py T1 18**

**root@BeagleBone:~# ./my_dump.py**

**t     n     v**

**2015-03-12 20:23:50     T1     18**

> Note that, by default, the MySQLdb library needs to execute these Python programs (which are not installed in the BeagleBone Black's filesystem), so you should add them using the following command:
>
> root@BeagleBone:~# aptitude install python-mysqldb

# Writing a custom daemon

As seen earlier, our BeagleBone Black has a lot of ready-to-use software, and a lot of readily available daemons that are useful for a lot of different tasks. However, we are developers, and if we have to develop some controlling or monitoring systems, it's quite normal that we should need a custom daemon to do our custom job.

In this last section, we'll see how to write our own daemon in several programming languages using a daemon skeleton that can be used to develop really complex daemons. Due to a lack of space, I cannot add all the possible features a daemon has, but the presented skeletons will have whatever you need to know about the daemon's creation.

All the example codes will implement a daemon with the following command line usage:

```
usage: mydaemon [-h] [-d] [-f] [-l]

    -h      - show this message

    -d      - enable debugging messages
```

```
-f      - do not daemonize
-l      - log on stderr
```

The -h option argument will show the help message, while the -d option argument will enable the debugging messages. The -f option argument will prevent the daemon from running in the background, and the -l option will print the logging messages to the standard error channel too. Apart from the -h option argument, the others are very useful during the debugging stages; in fact, if all are used together in the following form:

```
# ./mydaemon -d -f -l
```

The developer can run the daemon in the foreground with the enabled and printed debugging messages on the current terminal.

# Using C

In C language, a daemon skeleton can be written in the `chapter_11/mydaemon/my_daemon.c` file in the book's example code repository. The most important steps here are the `openlog()` call and the `daemon_body()` functions. In fact, the two `signal()` system calls are used to set up the signal handlers, while the whole job is done by the `daemon()` function call (see the beginning of this chapter). Here is the relevant code:

```c
/* Open the communication with syslogd */
loglevel = LOG_PID;
if (logstderr)
        loglevel |= LOG_PERROR;
openlog(NAME, loglevel, LOG_USER);

/* Install the signals traps */
sig_h = signal(SIGTERM, sig_handler);
if (sig_h == SIG_ERR) {
        fprintf(stderr, "unable to catch SIGTERM");
        exit(-1);
}
sig_h = signal(SIGINT, sig_handler);
if (sig_h == SIG_ERR) {
        fprintf(stderr, "unable to catch SIGINT");
        exit(-1);
}
dbg("signals traps installed");

/* Should run as a daemon? */
if (daemonize) {
        ret = daemon(!daemonize, 1);
```

```
        if (ret) {
                fprintf(stderr, "unable to daemonize the process");
                exit(-1);
        }
}

    daemon_body();
```

Now we can compile the code using `make`, and then we can execute it using the following command line:

**root@BeagleBone:~# ./mydaemon**

**root@BeagleBone:~#**

We notice that nothing happens since the prompt is returned. However, if we take a look at the system log files, we can see the daemon's activity:

**root@BeagleBone:~# tail -f /var/log/syslog**

**Mar 19 17:09:22 BeagleBone mydaemon[32368]: I'm working hard!**

**Mar 19 17:09:23 BeagleBone mydaemon[32368]: I'm working hard!**

**Mar 19 17:09:24 BeagleBone mydaemon[32368]: I'm working hard!**

# Using PHP

In PHP, creating a daemon is a bit more complex, as there is no dedicated function to daemonize a running process. However, the task is still quite simple, as shown in the `chapter_11/mydaemon/my_daemon.php` file in the book's example code repository. As for the C example, the important steps are done after the `openlog()` function call. The `pcntl_signal()` function is used to install the signal handlers, while the daemon is created using the `pcntl_fork()`, `exit()`, `chdir()`, and `fclose()` functions, as we have already explained this at the beginning of this chapter. Here is the code snippet:

```php
    openlog(NAME, $loglevel, LOG_USER);

    # Install the signals traps
    pcntl_signal(SIGTERM, "sig_handler");
    pcntl_signal(SIGINT,  "sig_handler");
    dbg("signals traps installed");

    # Start the daemon
    if ($daemonize) {
```

```
dbg("going in background...");
$pid = pcntl_fork();
if ($pid < 0) {
        die("unable to daemonize!");
}
if ($pid) {
        # The parent can exit...
        exit(0);
}
# ... while the children goes on!

# Set the working directory to /
chdir("/");

# Close all of the standard file descriptors as we are running
# as a daemon
fclose(STDIN);
fclose(STDOUT);
fclose(STDERR);
}

daemon_body();
```

In this case, the daemon can be executed using the command line:

**root@BeagleBone:~# ./mydaemon.php**

We get the same output as before.

# Using Python

In Python, the task is easier, as in C, as we have a dedicated library to daemonize the running process.

 To install a dedicated library and to create a daemon process in Python, we have to use the following command:

root@BeagleBone:~# aptitude install python-daemon

The code is in the `chapter_11/mydaemon/my_daemon.py` file in the book's example code repository. As before, the relevant part is after the `syslog.openlog()` method call. We simply create a dedicated context with the `daemon.DaemonContext()` method, and then within this context, we will execute our `daemon_body()` function. The relevant code is as follows:

```
# Open the communication with syslogd
loglevel = syslog.LOG_PID
if logstderr:
    loglevel |= syslog.LOG_PERROR
syslog.openlog(NAME, loglevel, syslog.LOG_USER)

# Define the daemon context and install the signals traps
context = daemon.DaemonContext(
    detach_process = daemonize,
)
context.signal_map = {
    signal.SIGTERM: sig_handler,
    signal.SIGINT: sig_handler,
}
dbg("signals traps installed")

# Start the daemon
with context:
    daemon_body()
```

The daemon is launched by the command line:

```
root@BeagleBone:~# ./mydaemon.py
```

# Using Bash

As the last example, I present you the daemon implementation of a Bash script. This example is not so relevant as the previous ones, since it is very rare to implement a daemon as a Bash script. However, it's interesting to show you how the Bash scripting can be powerful.

The Bash demon code is reported in the `chapter_11/mydaemon/my_daemon.sh` file in the book's example code repository. In this case, the relevant code is after the `trap` command, which is used to install the signals handler, and it's all concentrated into the line with the `eval` command. The `daemon_body()` function is called in such a way that the **stdin** and **stdout** channels are redirected to the `/dev/null` file, while the **stderr** channel is redirected if no options are supplied. Meanwhile, the background or foreground execution mode is selected by the respective command-line option argument. The relevant code is as follows:

```
# Install the signals traps
trap sig_handler SIGTERM SIGINT
dbg "signals traps installed"

# Start the daemon
if [ -n "$daemonize" ] ; then
    dbg "going in background..."

    # Set the working directory to /
    cd /
fi
[ -z "$logstderr" ] && tmp="2>&1"
eval daemon_body </dev/null >/dev/null $tmp $daemonize
```

In this case, we can run the daemon in the debugging mode, and then take a look at its output directly on the terminal:

```
root@BeagleBone:~# ./mydaemon.sh -d -f -l
mydaemon.sh: signals traps installed
mydaemon.sh: start main loop
mydaemon.sh: I'm working hard!
mydaemon.sh: I'm working hard!
mydaemon.sh: I'm working hard!
```

# Summary

Well, now you should be ready to use the *ready-to-use* daemons presented here, as far as writing your own daemon is concerned.

Using these example codes and the device's usage in the previous chapters, you should be able to realize a great project with the BeagleBone Black.

# Index

## Symbols

**1-Wire bus**
  about 179, 180
  electrical lines 181
  in Linux 181-184
  URL 181
**1-Wire devices**
  access, obtaining to 184-186
  URL 184

## A

**ADC (Analog to Digital Converter) 145**
**ADC chip 154-157**
**Ain pin 157**
**Apache web server 8-10**
**API (application programming interface) 75**
**armhf version 60**

## B

**Bash**
  LED, managing 88-94
  URL, for tutorial 94
  using 206, 207
**basic system management 35**
**BeagleBone Black**
  about 1
  Debian, installing 21
  developing system, setting up 10-13
  first login 4, 5
  GPIOs 76-78
  hardware key features 2-4
  pins 177

  preloaded tools 6
  system overview 2
  URL 169
  URL, for support page 147
**block device 99**
**Bone101 service**
  about 10
  reference 10
**bootcmd command 45**
**bootloader**
  about 42
  environment 44-47
  GPIOs management 43, 44
  kernel command line 49, 50
  SPL 42
  storage devices, managing 47-49
  U-Boot 42

## C

**C language**
  used, for writing custom daemon 203
**capes 4**
**char device 99**
**char driver 120**
**Chip Select (CS) 161**
**communication parameters 120**
**control lines**
  URL 118
**crontab 194, 195**
**custom daemon**
  writing 202
  writing, Bash used 206, 207
  writing, C used 203
  writing, PHP used 205
  writing, Python used 205

## Thank you for buying
# BeagleBone Essentials

## About Packt Publishing

Packt, pronounced 'packed', published its first book, *Mastering phpMyAdmin for Effective MySQL Management*, in April 2004, and subsequently continued to specialize in publishing highly focused books on specific technologies and solutions.

Our books and publications share the experiences of your fellow IT professionals in adapting and customizing today's systems, applications, and frameworks. Our solution-based books give you the knowledge and power to customize the software and technologies you're using to get the job done. Packt books are more specific and less general than the IT books you have seen in the past. Our unique business model allows us to bring you more focused information, giving you more of what you need to know, and less of what you don't.

Packt is a modern yet unique publishing company that focuses on producing quality, cutting-edge books for communities of developers, administrators, and newbies alike. For more information, please visit our website at www.packtpub.com.

## About Packt Open Source

In 2010, Packt launched two new brands, Packt Open Source and Packt Enterprise, in order to continue its focus on specialization. This book is part of the Packt Open Source brand, home to books published on software built around open source licenses, and offering information to anybody from advanced developers to budding web designers. The Open Source brand also runs Packt's Open Source Royalty Scheme, by which Packt gives a royalty to each open source project about whose software a book is sold.

## Writing for Packt

We welcome all inquiries from people who are interested in authoring. Book proposals should be sent to author@packtpub.com. If your book idea is still at an early stage and you would like to discuss it first before writing a formal book proposal, then please contact us; one of our commissioning editors will get in touch with you.

We're not just looking for published authors; if you have strong technical skills but no writing experience, our experienced editors can help you develop a writing career, or simply get some additional reward for your expertise.

## Learning BeagleBone

ISBN: 978-1-78398-290-5       Paperback: 206 pages

Learn how to love and care for your BeagleBone and teach it tricks

1. Develop the practical skills that are required to create an embedded Linux system using BeagleBone.

2. Use the embedded Linux software to control LEDs on the BeagleBone, empowering you to create LED flash patterns.

3. A hands-on guide, supported by practical examples to integrate BeagleBone into your projects.

## Getting Started with Electronic Projects

ISBN: 978-1-78355-451-5       Paperback: 176 pages

Build thrilling and intricate electronic projects using LM555, ZigBee, and BeagleBone

1. Get acquainted with fundamental concepts such as tools and circuits required for the projects.

2. Develop stunning cost-effective projects and build your own range of designs including flashlights, beacons, motion alarms, and wireless network alarm sensors using the LM555 timer, ZigBee, and BeagleBone.

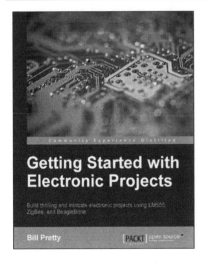

Please check **www.PacktPub.com** for information on our titles